If You Can't Quit Cryin', You Can't Come Here No More

A Family's Legacy of Poverty, Crime and
Mental Illness in Rural America

BETTY FRIZZELL

FERAL HOUSE

Dedication

This book is dedicated to Mom, Vicky, Julian,
and the love of my life, Gary "Wedge" Thompson.

Mom, Vicky and me, Poplar Bluff, Missouri, 1980

Mom wouldn't hold me like the mothers I saw on television. She didn't like to be touched or touch anyone else. She would say, "Stop that. You are all right," with maybe a slight pat on the back if I fell down or experienced one of the many emotional bruisings that cause kids to cry. After years of getting no response from Mom to my crying, I conditioned myself to cry silently and later not to cry, or for that matter, to not show emotion in any circumstance. However, since May 12, 2013, I have cried more than at any other time in my life.

As my then-husband Jimmy turned off the ten o'clock news, I realized my older sister, Vicky, hadn't called today. She lived 150 miles south of St. Louis in Puxico, Missouri—the "bootheel" of the state. Vicky didn't use social media or texting, so phone calls were our primary communication. I sat in bed and knew I couldn't sleep until I spoke to her. I called her. The phone rang, and her 30-year-old son, Kenny, answered.

"Where's Vicky at?" I said.

"Where the hell do you think she is? She's in Stoddard County Jail," he replied. "What for?" I asked.

"She killed Chris." He replied as if my sister murdering her husband was common knowledge, something I should've already known.

I hung up and screamed at Jimmy to get me the number for Stoddard County, Missouri Jail. He bolted straight up in bed.

"Why do you need the number for? What's going on?"

"Vicky killed Chris." Those words slipped out of my mouth, but they weren't my words. Someone in my body was saying them. I didn't want to own them.

"What? What happened?"

I stood there dialing the jail number and hoping Kenny was wrong. "Yes, do you have an inmate named Victoria Isaac?" I asked.

"Yeah. We have Victoria Isaac," the voice on the other end said.

"What's she in jail for?" I asked, praying it was for anything but murder.

"First-degree murder—no bond."

My legs went out from under me. As I sat stunned on the floor, Jimmy took the phone to speak to the deputy working the late-night shift answering calls. My heartbeat thrummed in my ears. I couldn't see the room through my tears.

"Calm down, honey. Calm down." Jimmy, always with high anxiety, couldn't stop talking. He went across the hallway and woke up my teenage son, Julian. Jimmy and Julian were speaking to me, but our world was stuck in slow motion. I was a cop down to the tips of my toes and as part of my police training, I understood how adrenaline works and how time stops during extreme stress. But this was my sister, not some random call from someone I didn't know. I felt dissociated from my own body, and I heard, again and again, ringing throughout my scattered and shattered thoughts, my mother's deathbed request to me: *"Take care of Vicky and Kenny because they ain't right."*

The Frizzell family. Back Row: Vesta and Victoria
Middle Row: Oscar, Grandpa Leander, Grandma Lottie, Jessie
Front: Roxie
.

$\mathcal{V}$icky isn't the first person in my family to be charged with felony murder. Murder is generational in our family. The Frizzells were known for two things: musical talent and quick tempers. Mom would describe her kin as the kind of people who "would rather shoot you than look at you." They played old-time country music as feverishly as they fought. As a child, I watched Grandma Roxie play the guitar with her brother Toots who played the left-handed fiddle while Aunt Lottie occasionally accompanied on the autoharp. My great-grandfather, Lee Frizzell, was the thirteenth of fourteen children born in Putnam County, Ohio. Lee married Lottie Carles in 1894 and started a family. Six years later, Lee moved the family in a covered wagon from northwestern Ohio to southeast Missouri. Lee and Lottie's seventh child, my grandmother Roxie, was born as the family crossed the Black River. They settled outside of Poplar Bluff, Missouri, on a plot of land near that very same river.

An old family story tells how a Black family with two small children, a boy and a girl, moved downriver from the Frizzell homestead. The children would play on the logs cut down to make the family's cabin and often strayed onto great-grandfather's land. Lee repeatedly told them to stay on their own property. One day, Lee and my elementary-school-aged grandmother Roxie saw the two children playing inside a hollowed-out log on a hill near the water's edge. Lee told Roxie to hide behind a tree while he took care of them "once and for all." He waited for the children to climb inside the log, then pushed the log down the hill and watched as it rolled into the water. With her hair ribbons blowing in the wind, Roxie stood silently as Lee walked to the river's edge and held that log, with the children trapped inside, under the water until the bubbles and water splashing stopped. Their parents would find the two bodies floating in the dark river a few hours later. Lee never denied or admitted causing their deaths. The police did not investigate. That's the kind of man he was.

Roxie lived with violence and had developed a taste for it as she grew older. An incident in February 1922 turned her heart as cold and dark as the Black River. Her older brother Jessie was deep in the woods making illegal alcohol. A man attempted to rob him. A fight ensued, but Jessie got free and ran toward the family's small cabin. Roxie, who had been out in the woods shooting squirrels, saw her brother running along the path. He told her to stop the man chasing him while he ran to get their father.

She stood silently behind a tree, wrapped her small hands around the gun, and fired a shot into the unknown pursuer. The man lay bleeding on the ground. Roxie held the gun over him until the brother and father arrived. Lee told her to go home and they would take care of the matter. No word was ever spoken about the incident. Days later, Roxie read a newspaper article that reported that a man's torso had been found floating in Black River and that the arms and legs had been severed clean off. The head was also missing and later discovered a short distance downriver. It, too, was maimed beyond all recognition.

10

Great-Uncle Lee (Toots), Grandma Roxie and me in 1981

You could say that homicidal ideation seemed to be genetic as the thread of violence running through the Frizzell bloodline was present in all my great-uncles, aunts, mother, and siblings. Roxie's older brother, my great-uncle, also named Lee, was arrested for murder on June 18, 1969. That night Lee had laid down in his bedroom to nap after a bout of heavy drinking. The noise of his step-grandchildren woke him. He loaded a gun and began randomly shooting through the closed door into the front room. His 17-year-old step-granddaughter was left dead, and his 13-year-old step-grandson was injured. He was charged with first-degree murder and sent to a psychiatric institution for three years. Her sister, Victoria, was infamous in Poplar Bluff. She was a madam who ran the establishment called "House of the Pleasurable Ladies." Another great-uncle, James, disappeared after being implicated in a series of murders in Washington state. He was never seen or heard from after that.

11

Even my Mom, as she lay on her deathbed in 2001, confessed to her involvement in several unnatural deaths. She told of how she and an older woman she called Aunt Pearl used to "roll" men for money.

During the 1950s, the east side of Poplar Bluff had a red-light district frequented by the men changing trains between St. Louis and Memphis. Aunt Pearl and Mom went to the downtown bars and lured men outside with the promise of sex. They would take the men for a ride out into the country and, once isolated and alone, one of them would knock the man unconscious then steal his money. They'd leave him at the side of the road to walk the many miles back to town when he came to.

On one particular evening, a victim overwhelmed them during the heist and began beating Mom. Aunt Pearl always tucked a blackjack into her dress. She hit the man near his temple with all her strength and killed him. They loaded the body into the car and drove to the old Frizzell family graveyard. They found the fresh grave, that of a distant cousin, and opened it back up. Mom and Pearl threw the dead body into the hole with the coffin then shoveled the dirt back in. No one missed an unknown transient, let alone searched for him in a backwoods cemetery in rural Missouri.

Mom's mercurial temper led to another incident that took place near the Dam at Lake Wappapello. Mom and a random man had been out drinking all night long. For reasons lost to time, Mom was drunkenly driving them down the highway as they began to argue, and, in a rage, she tried to kill them both by driving into Lake Wappapello. At the last moment, she swerved and hit the rocks that line Highway T on the lake's eastern shore. The truck flipped. As she crawled out of the wreckage, the bleeding man threw a final punch that blackened her eye. In her drunken rage, she stood on his chest as he bled out and died. She stumbled miles down the road to a payphone and called her sister to pick her up, never once mentioning the dead man.

The Frizzell violent streak was in us kids too. My oldest sister Jackie was affiliated with motorcycle gangs and had multiple arrests because of her connection to several mysterious gang-related deaths. She escaped conviction in each incident. The June 1978 killing of her ex-husband and father of her children is still unsolved. The body had been found in a dump in Wyoming covered with milk cartons, dog food, and miscellaneous garbage in the hope to speed up decomposition of the body. He had been shot twice, execution-style, with a .22 caliber handgun. I can go on. There are more stories of aunts, uncles, and cousins who were perpetrators of violent acts large and small, while also victims of an endless and multi-generational cycle of poverty and mental illness. Now my sister Vicky, who was closest to me in age and least able to care for herself, was in jail and charged with killing her husband.

I'm a Missouri country girl. The way I was raised, when your mom told you to jump, you didn't sass back; you jumped. When Mom was dying during the summer of 2001, confessing stories of her dark past, every request she made felt important. I thought it would be dishonorable not to go to any length to follow her commands, no matter how impossible. Oftentimes, I wished I was raised somewhere else, somewhere the burden of my raisin' didn't have a hold over me. Friends from other parts of the United States didn't understand my devotion to my Mom—a woman I didn't understand or even like.

How can I explain how we loved and feared our Mom? Psychologists today use the term "trauma bonding," but as a kid growing up during the '70s and '80s, there were no terms for Mom's constant yet unstable presence in our lives. It was our *normal*. Violence from the hands of your family was to be expected, but if outsiders dare threaten us, that was another thing altogether and would be met eye for an eye. Loyalty to our blood and kin was bred in the bone, and to disobey my Mom would be to betray that sacred bond. Mom's last words haunted me—*"Take care of Vicky and Kenny because they ain't right."* It wasn't so much out of love that I would fulfill my promise to take care of Vicky and Kenny, but out of duty.

13

CHAPTER ONE

On the phone, Kenny explained his recollection of the day's events in a very matter-of-fact manner in his thick Southern drawl. He woke up early that morning and walked to a nearby convenience store. Vicky had asked him to buy her lottery tickets. After returning from the store, he sat down with Vicky at the kitchen table and drank his coffee. She collected her lottery tickets and went back to her bedroom at the front of the trailer while Chris slept on the living room couch.

In Kenny's telling, he went to his bedroom at the other end of the trailer and fell asleep. A short time later, he was awakened by the sound of six gunshots. Kenny didn't see Vicky reload the gun with bullets from a box kept on top of the refrigerator but says that she did it. He said that he ran into the living room to see Vicky, standing only a few feet from Chris' sleeping body on the couch, fire two bullets from our Mom's old .22 caliber handgun into Chris' head. Then Vicky tried to turn the gun on herself.

He said that he yelled to stop her, telling her to drop the gun. And then she threw it down, picked up her phone, and called 911 to tell the operator that she shot her husband. Then she handed the phone to Kenny.

Kenny described Vicky as "not having any life in her face." When the police arrived, Kenny was taken to Puxico Police Department, and Vicky was taken to the Stoddard County Sheriff's Department. After the local police interrogated Kenny for a few hours, they brought him back to the trailer—an active crime scene—and left him alone in the filth and blood.

I listened to Kenny's recitation of the events, but something about the story didn't seem right. As I calmed down, I heard the story in a new way—the way a cop hears it. Because of, or maybe in spite of, my family's century-long criminal history, I made my career in law enforcement. Every police officer is taught from the first day of training that if a situation doesn't feel right, and a

15

story doesn't sound plausible, it isn't. And the story I heard wasn't making any sense.

The murder weapon, Mom's old .22 pistol, was a gun I knew well because I had held it, loaded it, and shot it during the many hours I spent at the shooting range practicing for the police qualifying test. I knew that gun. It was a cheap gun, which meant that it had a heavy trigger pull and slow, rough action. It would have taken a fair amount of time for Vicky to shoot six rounds, walk across the room, get the bullets from the box on top of the refrigerator, reload at least four more rounds, and finally shoot twice until, as Kenny stated to the Sheriff's deputy, he saw her turn the gun on herself.

The sound of the first shot would have been as loud as a bomb going off inside that metal-sided trailer. For someone, anyone, to sleep through gunfire tens of feet away would be nearly impossible, let alone someone who was known to be a light sleeper.

No, this wasn't adding up. There was more to the story.

"Were they fighting?" Jimmy asked Kenny as they continued talking on the phone.

"No, they were getting along real good. They'd borrowed some money the day before and got their prescriptions filled," Kenny said.

The word "prescriptions" angered the cop in me. Southeast Missouri is a home for "Doctor Feelgoods" and crooked pain management clinics that over-prescribe opioids.[1] I can't count the number of arrests for prescription pill abuse I have witnessed in my career.

Southeast Missouri, the "bootheel" of the state, south of the confluence of the Ohio and Mississippi Rivers, is an impoverished area with few employment opportunities aside from factory farming and manufacturing work. This was a part of the country where a Social Security disability check is the primary income source. In 2013, in Puxico, a population of 873 people, the Social Security administration recorded that 830 people collected some kind of

---

1 "Missouri Is a Pill Lover's Paradise." Vice, July 28, 2014.

government benefits[2]. Meaning, only 43 people in the township earned their living solely from work-generated income.

Once on Social Security, a person qualifies for medical assistance, which is often the only way for the poor and working poor to access healthcare. But unscrupulous doctors could fatten their pockets by prescribing more and more pills to get more money through the Medicare/Medicaid reimbursements and incentives from the pharmaceutical companies. Daily in the newspapers, we now read how Perdue Pharma's sales campaign to doctors led many people to addiction and to doctor-shopping. A person could visit multiple physicians who would each prescribe an opioid drug. Pharmacies would fill these scripts with little to no oversight, so much so that in late 2020 the United States Department of Justice sued Walmart[3] because their pharmacies were so lackadaisical in following abuse prevention mandates, and filled fraudulent prescriptions.

The giant corporations, drug manufacturers, and corrupt doctors were making enough money to turn a blind eye to the impact these drugs had on rural communities eager to escape from the despair of their daily lives. Social Security checks were issued on the third and fifteenth of the month, but you didn't need a calendar to mark those dates; you could see people lined up by the hundreds outside every pharmacy door waiting for bags of prescription opiates.

Selling prescription medicine has long been a side business for a person getting the drugs. As a child, even though at the time I didn't know what it was, I watched Mom sell her prescriptions for extra money to get us through until the end of the month. Then the cycle of Social Security checks and script refills starts all over again.

The drug abuse was just part of Vicky's issues. Whatever intellectual and social capacity she had was diminished by a hemorrhagic stroke in May of 2012. Since the stroke, her personality had changed from a tough and confident woman to that of an addled child. The internal brain bleed caused changes to her mental and psychological state. She often called me—up to 20 times a day—

2 Social Security Administration report, 2013
3 United States Justice Department press release titled, "Department of Justice Files Nationwide Lawsuit Against Walmart Inc. for Controlled Substances Act Violations'. December 20, 2020.

sometimes talking in a childlike voice. One day she called and rambled for an hour about how the sky opened up and invited her into heaven. And another time, she left a nonsensical voicemail about a conversation she had with the cardinal bird decoration on our dead mother's clock. I was so troubled by Vicky's deteriorating mental state that in late 2012 I consulted an attorney about putting Vicky into my legal guardianship to protect her from Chris, the drugs, and from a lifestyle she was no longer capable of sustaining.

In early 2013, Vicky and Chris were going from doctor to doctor getting prescriptions. They would make up ailments or injuries to get more medications from complicit providers. They both used and sold opiates as a matter of generating extra cash and helping fellow addicts. Vicky had prided herself on being a good driver, but once the prescription drug abuse started after her marriage to Chris, she had a series of car wrecks. It was the beginning of what would become known as the "opioid crisis." Due to my police training, I recognized their behavior as full-on prescription drug abuse.

Jimmy continued to listen to Kenny's memories of Vicky and Chris' relationship, but I didn't want to hear any more. As soon as I heard the word "prescriptions," I got disgusted and went downstairs. I stumbled to my computer and started searching for news coverage of Chris' murder that morning.

One online article read:

"A man is dead and his wife charged with murder after an early morning shooting in Puxico. Stoddard County Sheriff Carl Hefner on Tuesday afternoon said Victoria Isaac, the victim's 48-year-old wife, of Puxico, was charged with first-degree murder."[4]

And another:

"Missouri woman said something told her to end him."[5]

I was apprehensive when Kenny moved into Vicky's tiny, three-bedroom mobile home earlier in April, about a month before the

4 https://www.semissourian.com/story/1968915.html
5 https://www.kfvs12.com/story/22247133/1-dead-1-in-custody-in-stoddard-county/

murder. He had been evicted from the house he'd rented for the past eight years, since he was 22 years old. He never told us a reason for the eviction. Vicky was eager to show Kenny how much she loved him and invited him to move in. The addition of her 30-year-old, 6'6", muscular, tattooed son to the household was a disaster in the making as Kenny already had a history of violence toward Vicky and Chris.

Within two weeks of moving in, Kenny got mad at Vicky for some unknown thing. He towered over her with his large hands and strangled her, leaving hand-mark-shaped bruises on both sides of her neck. Although the police were called, no arrests were made. Not long after that incident, Chris punched Kenny and blackened his right eye. Kenny called 911 and told the operator that he was going to kill Vicky and Chris. When the officers arrived, Kenny was in the front yard telling the police he planned to kill Vicky, Chris, and then himself. The police took him to the local hospital's psychiatric ward for observation. He was released two days later in early May. Less than a week later, Chris was murdered. Yet the police didn't think Kenny was involved? Even after threatening to kill them days before?

The news article[6] had a summary of the "probable cause statement." The probable cause statement is a document written by the police listing the facts of a case and applying for and justifying an arrest warrant. The statement said that at 8:18 a.m., Vicky called 911 to report she had shot and killed her husband. The report noted that Chris was shot six times. Vicky was arrested and advised of her Miranda rights. She told the officer she took medications that morning before the shooting. The report stated that she was "just laying in bed and 'something' told her to get up and 'end him.'" Vicky was going to "end herself," but her son came into the room, causing her not to have enough time to load the rounds to commit suicide.

The statements attributed to Vicky made no sense to me.

Vicky would never commit suicide. We were Southern Baptist, and the church taught us suicide is self-murder and punishable

---

6 https://www.kfvs12.com/story/22247133/1-dead-1-in-custody-in-stoddard-county/

by an eternity in hell. Mom didn't go to services, but she made sure we were on a bus headed to Sunday school every week. Vicky loved the Lord; even when she wasn't living right, her faith was important. Even thinking about suicide is a sin; there is no redemption, only judgment in heaven.

In no uncertain terms, Vicky wanted to go to heaven because she believed that she would see Mom again. Vicky tried hard to live her life in a Christian manner and would often say, "I am gonna see my Mommy again." In the Southern tradition, you might wish to God for death to bring you home to heaven, but you would never commit suicide. Even at her lowest moments, Vicky never talked of killing herself because she couldn't be reunited with Mom if she was in hell.

Something was definitely wrong with the story Kenny and the police were telling.

The mugshot of Vicky posted online didn't look like her. I didn't know the person in the picture. She wore my sister's face but looked distant, sad, and disoriented. Hard living had aged her, but I always saw Vicky as a young, spirited, music-loving girl who dreamed of being Stevie Nicks. She would listen to Fleetwood Mac for hours as she twirled around singing, *Rhiannon—she rules her life like a bird in flight.*

Vicky was born in 1965 and was the second youngest of us eight kids; I was six years younger. All of us experienced physical abuse as a regular part of our everyday lives—in our house, getting walloped by Mom was as common as brushing our teeth or putting our shoes on. We came to expect it, but Vicky was different. It was as if she couldn't stop herself from fighting back.

Disobedience was disrespectful—that was the biggest insult you could give Mom. No one, especially her children, talked back to her. If she even sensed defiance to her will, she responded with smacks and punches until you obediently submitted to her. Vicky's inability to regulate her feelings, temper, and behavior led

20

Vicky as a child, Poplar Bluff, Missouri 1977

to constant conflict in our house. The first decades of her life were spent beaten and bruised. Mom started to beat her for the merest of perceived slights she believed were disrespecting her authority. I clearly remember an incident when Vicky was ten years old that happened when we were sitting down at the table for dinner and someone spilled gravy on the white cloth tablecloth. Mom's first thought was Vicky had done it when it was actually our older sister, Sylvie.

21

"Did you do that?" Mom asked.

"No, it wasn't me," Vicky said.

"Then who was it?" Mom asked.

Vicky sat and looked ahead.

"Who was it? Don't you fuckin' hear me? I ain't asking you again."

Vicky remained silent. I waited for my cowardly older sister Sylvie to say something.

Mom slapped Vicky across the face twice. The intensity of her blows grew with each hit.

"You ignoring me?" Mom said, as she pulled Vicky by her hair out of the chair and started kicking her.

"Say somethin'. Fuckin' say something," Mom yelled as she kicked Vicky in the ribs.

Vicky didn't cry; she lay on the floor, taking the beating. Mom soon stopped, but Vicky lay on the floor unresponsive and bleeding.

"Get your inconsiderate ass to your room," Mom yelled.

Vicky didn't move. My older sisters helped her to her feet and pushed her to the bedroom.

"Why does she make me do these things to her?" Mom asked me. I shook my head and shrugged my shoulders as I stood terrified and frozen behind the chair.

Our large family wasn't close. Never was. Mom distrusted affection and love as a weakness. She tried to raise us to be like her—tough. We weren't raised as much as we were trained like dogs for pit fighting, to defend ourselves and protect what was ours. Each of my siblings turned out to be vastly different people.

All of them were named after Mom's relatives, except me; I was named after the first woman mayor of Poplar Bluff, Betty Absheer. As a little girl reading about her accomplishments in the newspaper, I felt a sense of pride being named for such an incredible woman. She carried herself with quiet confidence and a sense of humor.

She also came from the impoverished east side of Poplar Bluff and rose to one of the highest local government positions.

Mom separated me from the rest of the family in more ways than just my name. I have nothing in common and no bond with the rest of them, only with Vicky. I felt like a stranger who stood by witnessing abuse.

Vicky and I should be more alike considering we're the two youngest of the eight kids, but we were as different as night and day. In every family, there are designated roles that become part of the dynamic of how the relationships develop and how siblings interact with their parents and each other. I was born with a "veil" on my face (sometimes called "born in the caul") and was the youngest so Mom decided that I was gifted with intelligence, destined for great things and that I had a mysterious supernatural power of "seeing."

Mom used to say, "Betty is smart because she knows things we don't or can't know." This mystical expectation to always be good and smart bred in me the obsessive-compulsive disorder of moral scrupulosity. I wanted everything in its place and a place for everything. I couldn't control my chaotic, unstable home, but I could use rituals to regulate other parts of my life. In first grade, the teacher scolded me for not finishing a coloring project that I didn't even start due to the fact that I had to rearrange the box of 64 crayons in order of darkest to lightest. The years of watching Mom fight and hurt people made me work even harder to be more than a compassionate person; I wanted to be perfect.

Vicky's role in the family was the "bad seed." She was academically inferior to her classmates and overweight. The school told Mom that she also had a "conduct disorder." Kids at school, and even our sister Sylvie, bullied Vicky and called her names like "fat and retarded." Despite her difficulty learning, Vicky excelled at athletics and singing in the choir. Mom always asked her why she couldn't stay out of trouble. Her usual answer was, "I don't know. I guess I'm just bad."

One thing Vicky and I did have in common was not knowing the identity of our biological fathers. Mom had eight children from five different men. At least our other siblings knew who their respective fathers were, but Vicky and I were not allowed to ask about ours. Our father, for all intents and purposes, was Mom's last husband, Aubrey Pickard. I don't remember much about him as he died when I was about six years old. When I asked about a "dad," Mom would say, "I am your father and your mother. That is all you need to know."

For the first nine years of my life, my name was Betty Hurley. This was the name I learned how to spell and write in kindergarten. Mom said changing names was easy because she had many last names. She had at least three Social Security cards with three different names. I was in the third grade when my name changed too. It was the day of the school Halloween party, and after the party we paraded through the town. It was a big day, and I forgot my costume at home. I called Mom and asked her to bring the outfit to school.

She agreed, and while driving her Ford LTD to school, she rear-ended another Ford LTD, pushing that car into oncoming traffic. Which caused it to hit another Ford LTD. Mom didn't have any car insurance. She would have lost her driver's license because of her multiple outstanding unpaid tickets. Mom blamed me for the wreck.

She pulled me aside and said, "Because of that wreck, you are going to help me with *my* Halloween costume." We went to the local United Gospel Rescue Mission thrift store. We bought a girdle, an old-fashioned cotton dress, an auburn wig, and large frame glasses. Mom didn't usually dress like this. She was never seen in a dress or without her red lipstick and nail polish, even if she was working in her garden or on a car. I thought there was some special Halloween for adults, and her costume was a church lady.

When we got home, Mom had me wash the wig out in fabric softener and helped me put curlers in it like playing with my dolls. The next day, I helped her put on the "Halloween costume" by

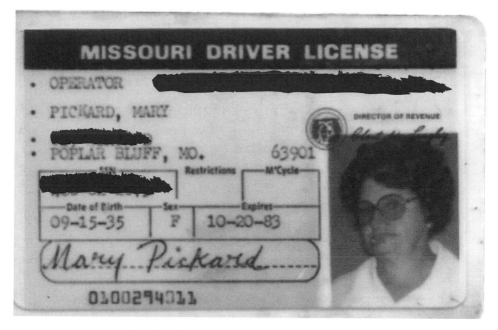

Mom's "Mary Pickard" driver's license

squeezing her into the girdle and pinning the wig in the back of her head. She kept me out of school during my first few hours of class and made me go with her to the license bureau. She did this because the glasses weren't the right prescription and made things blurry—I had to be her eyes. As we arrived at the motor vehicle department, she took her dentures out and put them in her purse. We walked in, and I sat in the driver's testing waiting room while she took her driver's test. She passed while wearing those glasses by pulling them down to her nose and looking over the top of them.

After she was done, we got in the car and went home. If this was an adult Halloween party, it was the most boring party ever. A few weeks later, she got a new driver's license in the mail under the name Mary Pickard. Then we moved to the east side of Poplar

25

Bluff, and I started at a new school as Betty Pickard. I was told never to use the name Hurley again. Mom told the school that my records were changed because she didn't want her children to have different surnames.

People raised by nice people in nice homes often have difficulty believing that Mom really went to such lengths to avoid bills and responsibilities. Growing up, I thought our lives were normal. You get used to chaos when that's what you see every day.

School was a refuge for me, a safe place where my obsessive tendencies toward perfection were rewarded. Yet, the schools in rural Missouri during the '70s and '80s still used corporal punishment to "correct" bad attitudes and behavior. A school didn't need special permission from your parents to hit you because it was assumed that was how you were punished at home.

Our school was no exception. "Paddlings" consisted of having the child bend over to touch their toes and stand in that position while the teacher or principal struck their behind with a large wooden paddle. This was done in front of other students to add to the humiliation. I would see Vicky in the hallway waiting for the teacher to come out to administer the paddling. Mom would then get called by the school about Vicky disrupting class and have to come to pick her up. As soon as they got home, Mom would beat her again.

My teachers took an interest in me outside of school and encouraged me to use the mind I was given. I began to realize that there were different ways to live life. I saw people at church who could afford to put money in the collection plate without shame.

In junior high school, I started having vivid nightmares that I was a waitress living in rural Poplar Bluff in a double-wide trailer married to an abusive man. I was instinctively rejecting the lifestyle of my Mom and the people around her. The '70s/'80s television show *Alice* amplified those nightmares, as the comic relief and butt of jokes was a stereotypical man-crazy Southern

26

woman stuck in a dead-end job. I began to see that a rural way of life that rejected education and kept women oppressed was not for me. I wanted to see the world, play music, and not financially struggle. I wanted to be like those other people who wipe the white trash away from their DNA. I longed for a family, two children, a loving husband, and stability.

But Vicky was on a different path. Vicky came to believe that she deserved to be abused and that her life was destined to be a struggle. She dropped out of high school when she was 16 in 1981, having only completed the ninth grade. She grew a hard exterior that hid a kind, loving person. Mom's constant abuse warped Vicky's sense of what love is and what it looks like. For us, love came at the end of a fist.

Vicky never wanted to be a mother. She believed the doctors who told her that she could never conceive due to pelvic injuries sustained in a childhood bicycle accident. As teenagers, we were taught that sex was bad, and that's all we needed to know. Then Vicky got pregnant when she was 18 years old. She refused to believe it and wouldn't go to the doctor until Mom confronted her. Mom had been pregnant too many times and knew better. "Listen, you can sit here and lie, but you're big and pregnant. Now go to the doctor." She didn't seek medical treatment until she was in the ninth month.

Kenny's biological father, Kenneth Sr., wasn't prepared to be a parent either. He was 11 years older than Vicky, a tall, thin man called Kenmore by his family, after the diesel trucks he loved to drive. He had been recently discharged from the U.S. Army, where he served as a truck driver. They married just before their son, Kenneth (Kenny) Lee Smith II, was born on December 14, 1983. They lived together as a family in a small house off Main Street on the north side of Poplar Bluff, Missouri, until Kenny was about a year old. Things began to go wrong when Kenneth Sr. lost his job as an over-the-road truck driver after he came to work intoxicated and wrecked a company semi.

The small family then moved closer to his relatives in Hopkinsville, Kentucky. When he was sober, Kenneth Sr. was

27

Vicky and her first husband, Kenneth Sr. 1983

friendly and laid-back, but like Vicky, his personality changed when he drank, and he turned into a sloppy drunk. The marriage only lasted about six months when a drunk and angry Kenneth Sr. came home looking to beat on someone. Vicky was always that someone. The police came this time, and he landed in jail while Vicky made the two-hundred-some-mile midnight drive back home to Missouri. She arrived at Mom's house early the next morning, sporting a dark, black eye and a big bloody lip with little Kenny at her side.

Vicky didn't see Kenneth Sr. again for years, and Kenny only saw him a total of twice more after that. Even when Vicky moved back home with Kenny after being beaten by her then-husband, Mom didn't show her any kindness. Vicky tried hard to be a good mother, but Mom refused to allow it. Vicky worked two and three jobs like she was paying penance for being abused and moving back home. Vicky came home exhausted as she gave Mom every penny earned. Then Mom belittled her for being gone all the time. She told Vicky that she didn't deserve to be a mother, and it was her fault that Kenny was "slow." Vicky couldn't win for trying.

Mom was the first to realize that 18-month-old Kenny had learning difficulties. Potty training was impossible. He didn't understand simple concepts like colors and playing with toys. Kenny would open his mouth and shake his hands up and down like he was having alcohol detox tremors when overstimulated or frustrated. Mom called them his "bird calls" because he looked like the pigeons she used to raise.

"Betty, he just ain't right. But I'm going to make sure he survives this old world," Mom said.

We were all in this pressure cooker of a house together—Mom, teenage me, Vicky, and little Kenny—haunted by the demons of unresolved trauma and unrelenting pain of mental illness while trapped by hateful poverty. Vicky coped the way she saw Mom manage everything: by drinking. When Vicky drank, she became angry and violent—just like Mom. It was the same pattern as in our childhood, but this time, Vicky was the one binge-drinking, followed by run-ins with the police that put her in and out of jail. Mom replaced Vicky as Kenny's parent.

Mom was a familiar face in the dive bars of Poplar Bluff, so it wasn't surprising when a friendly bartender called to inform her that her daughter was getting the shit kicked out of her by two women and a couple of men. I still wasn't old enough to legally drive, but that didn't stop Mom from having me drive her to the bar to retrieve Vicky. She was half-conscious as she slumped in a chair in the corner. The bartender helped me rouse Vicky and convince her to stand up and leave. We got her into Mom's car, and then I drove Vicky's blue 1978 Camaro back to our house. That Camaro, icon of party-loving girls throughout the rural South,

Mom, Vicky and Kenny, Poplar Bluff, Missouri 1985

had been driven drunkenly throughout the county so that it was riddled with whiskey dents, and sported a broken steering column that exposed the ignition. I fitted the screwdriver into the column to start the car and got us safely home.

As soon as we got back to the house, I parked the Camaro and went to help Mom. I worked to get Kenny out of his car seat as Mom was getting out. Vicky calmly got out of the passenger side, walked over to the Camaro, hopped into the driver's seat then sped off to another bar. She did this kind of thing for the next six months. She acted like she was asking to die. It didn't take long before she was arrested for Driving While Intoxicated.

Vicky got out of jail and decided to settle down and try to be a real mother to Kenny, but Mom kept pushing her out of Kenny's

30

life. Mom told her, "You're not fit to be a mother. You did this to this baby. You dirty bitch... You'd be better off dead."

Vicky was friends with a family who owned a traveling carnival. She decided to travel with them with the idea of earning money for Mom and Kenny. Vicky felt if she gave Mom enough money, she would finally love and accept her. She ran the rides and operated games like basketball toss while traveling through Missouri, Arkansas, and Louisiana. She would go out on the carnival circuit for a few months at a time, returning home with less money than she expected. Vicky would stay for a little while before going back out on the road again.

I thought her nomadic lifestyle was scary, but Vicky found freedom. Freedom from Mom continually reminding her that she was a failure as a daughter and mother. A different town every night meant that she met new people who didn't have to know her past or who her family was and that no one loved her as she tore down the old broken-down carnival rides with the peeling paint and creaky wheels.

With Mom firmly in charge of her toddler son, Vicky came and went for the next few years. Each time she returned she had a new boyfriend in tow. They were dirty white boys, carnival workers with long hair, or criminals who had nicknames like Ducky Love. Each one had a different story but the common links of substance abuse and using Vicky as a punching bag. A skinny blond named Bones with drinking and anger issues brought her carnival days to an end when he gave her two black eyes and broke her nose in several places. The damage was so severe that it required reconstructive surgery.

This time Vicky stayed home and stopped drinking. She now qualified for Social Security disability income after being diagnosed with anxiety. Social Security meant a steady income, but it didn't mean a supportive mental health system. She just traded one addictive coping mechanism for another. She gave Mom most of

31

her SSI checks and would go on binges to play bingo or buy lottery tickets with her small allowance. She'd become obsessed to the point of pawning guns, tools, and anything of value around the house. The gambling binge would fade only to be replaced with a new obsession like raising farm animals, collecting dolls, or whatever seized her mind and temporarily soothed her broken soul.

Amid this turmoil, Vicky got pregnant by a younger guy. At first, she didn't let Mom know about the man. Vicky's boyfriends were usually bad news, but I was a naïve 16-year-old and had hoped he was a good person for her and Kenny. Mom, who was always critical of Vicky's choice of men, eventually found out about both the boyfriend and the pregnancy. Mom called me into the front room.

"Betty, Vicky is pregnant. I don't know what we are going to do. We don't need another baby to raise," she said.

"Well, does she want the baby? Or does she want to give it away or have an abortion?" I was scared even to say those words. Mom condemned abortion because of her religious and personal beliefs and boasted how she gave birth to eight babies, even if it was not during the best circumstances.

"I never in my life had an abortion. But she can't take care of the one she has. With her drinking, what if it turns out like Kenny or worse? I am too old to go through this."

"What does *she* want to do with the baby? She can give it up for adoption," I said.

"No. I don't want to see it. She needs to get rid of it."

Mom did not give Vicky a say in having this baby. The baby's father didn't want responsibility for the child. Mom used this fact to point out how stupid Vicky was and not capable of making good choices. She harangued and yelled until Vicky eventually agreed and consented to have an abortion.

The next week, I drove her to Cape Girardeau, where one of the two abortion clinics in Missouri was located. She didn't say much on the trip over. She just stared out the window. I turned up the radio and drove.

As we arrived at the clinic, we were met by a crowd of anti-abortion protesters. They began yelling about how we were going to hell and how murder was a sin. I looked at Vicky, and a single tear ran down her eye. I asked her, "Do you really want to go through with this?"

She stared ahead and said, "Yes, I have to."

"You don't have to. We can go home."

"No. Mom said we are doing this, and we are doing this," Vicky said in an angry tone like she was trying to convince herself more than me.

I stopped the car. Vicky got out. I asked her if she wanted me to go in with her.

"No, I got in this mess alone. I will get out of it by myself," and she walked into the clinic.

I waited outside for three hours and worked on my knitting for Home Ec class. A guy came up to me and asked why I was knitting booties for a baby that wasn't going to be born. I never thought of her having a baby. As usual, Vicky and I were doing as we were told and not questioning Mom's decision.

We never talked about the baby or her pregnancy again. About three months later, she got a complete hysterectomy. She lost a lot of blood and went into shock for three days.

Vicky was a lifelong wrestling fan. She started attending local shows. She began a friendship with a regionally famous wrestler from Memphis, Tennessee. He had been featured on the World Wrestling Entertainment (WWE) and World Championship Wrestling (WCW). He and his manager toured Missouri, Arkansas, and Tennessee, doing small shows. Vicky went to Memphis for a couple of weeks and trained with a former women's champion. She could have finally found her niche in life, but she began to have feelings for the man, who neglected to tell her he had a wife and children living in another state while he trained in Memphis. When Vicky found out, she was crushed. Vicky could not be the other woman. When Mom learned about the details of the affair, she didn't praise Vicky for her moral rectitude in not taking up with a married man but told her how incompetent she was in handling her own life.

Vicky, who was incredibly emotionally fragile, saw this as another failure, and abandoned her wrestling dreams, and started drinking again. She began to see a man named "Jamie," and the cycle of physical abuse returned to Vicky's life. It wasn't too long before she was arrested for another Driving While Intoxicated charge. But this time, the charge it came with additional charges of probation violation, which landed her in jail. Not just any jail—my jail where I was working as a young, rookie deputy sheriff. Every time I booked in another person, I had to see her covered in bruises while she sat waiting for her appearance before the judge. She was sentenced to serve 18 months at the Women's Eastern Reception, Diagnostic and Correctional Center in Vandalia, Missouri.

Fifteen-plus years of an endless series of abusive boyfriends and a broken heart were Vicky's "love life" until she met Chris Isaac in 2001. Like many people on a Saturday and Sunday night, you could find Mom in front of the television watching a wrestling program. Mom shared her love of the sports entertainment action and storylines with Kenny and Vicky. Mom began going to local wrestling events where she met Chris' older brother and fellow wrestling enthusiast, Elmer Isaac. Mom thought him a hard-working man who worked for years as a school janitor, and was impressed by his polite, respectful country mannerisms. In 2002, the Isaac family opened their own wrestling company and started putting on shows at the local National Guard Armory. Chris was one of the wrestlers. He was five years younger than Vicky when Mom introduced them. He was smitten. And why not? She had worked hard to stay in shape, was a fan and had trained as a wrestler, and read the Bible to change her life while in jail.

When Chris asked her out on a date, Vicky was reluctant. Mom told her to go, because "What could it hurt?" After a quick courtship and with Mom's approval, Vicky moved into his trailer 20 miles away in Puxico, Missouri. Mom liked Chris because she believed he was a good man like his brother, Elmer, but soon all of us, Mom included, started to see he was nothing like his brother.

Now Vicky sat in a small jail cell for possibly the rest of her life, and I wanted someone to blame. Mom was that person. She

34

taught Vicky helplessness, and now she would pay for that lesson by giving up her freedom for the rest of her life.

Nestled in southeast Missouri near the Arkansas border, Puxico was a dying town. It had no real industry or viable economic opportunities, and there was little chance to escape poverty. In the taverns, people engaged in quiet games of pool while older, traditional-style country music played in the background. A boxcar sat frozen in time on a broken railroad siding leading nowhere. Dozens of long, winding dirt roads snaked to unknown and unwelcoming locations. The streets were lined with old cars, the owners too poor to afford anything newer than a dozen years old. Vicky loved this community. She was a regular attendee of the annual Puxico Homecoming parade and fair, where she got her favorite treat—a goat burger. Vicky enjoyed watching the Miss Puxico Beauty Pageant, the Little Miss Puxico Beauty Pageant, and even the baby pageant.

Chris had lived in Puxico most of his life. At 31, he was five years younger than Vicky when they met. He was a stocky man with a large bridge nose and flowing brown hair cut in a perpetual mullet. He looked like one of the many late-1980s wrestlers he loved. It was the era of wrestling when the World Wrestling Federation and its newly minted stars became pop-culture celebrities via the television-hyped matches and new, more "soap opera" storylines that turned a physical competition into a complicated psychological drama.

Chris was the youngest of eight children and didn't like school. He struggled with a learning disability but managed to graduate from Puxico High School. He then bounced around jobs and racked up several brushes with the criminal justice system. When he and Vicky met, he had settled into a job at the Tyson Chicken factory, catching chickens as they were loaded off the truck. But that was just a job; his real passion was professional wrestling.

Vicky and Chris met as their social circles became intertwined on the small yet dedicated regional wrestling circuit. Chris' family opened their own wrestling performance company that featured Chris and other family members as they toured in Missouri and Arkansas playing at National Guard Armories and small venues barely big enough to fit a wrestling ring.

Chris had trouble differentiating between the scripted fights in the ring and real life. He often picked fights with other wrestlers, much to their surprise, when he met them at the grocery store or community events. He suffered injuries in the ring from wrestling with others like him who were poorly trained amateurs hoping to be discovered. Even with the sophisticated choreography and physical conditioning used at the premier levels of pro wrestling, injuries among wrestlers are common. For aspiring wrestlers grappling in less-than-ideal rings and matched against other amateurs, injuries were a daily event. Prescription opiates were the easiest way to stop the pain and continue wrestling.

Chris' family, the Isaacs, were like our family: eight kids, and most had criminal records. Unlike us, the Isaacs were close-knit, probably because their married parents were involved in their raising. One of the Isaac sisters broke free of the cycle of poverty and went to college to become a social worker, and married an equally stable man who was a school principal. But the other Isaacs either worked menial jobs or collected Social Security and other public assistance benefits. A few of Chris' siblings had convictions for theft and manufacturing methamphetamine.

The entire extended family lived the whole of their lives in the Bootheel area, which was insular and was part of the echo chamber that reinforced their conservative political view of anyone outside the area as a threat. I understood them. Even though I had lived in Europe and moved away from southeast Missouri, I understood their literal interpretation of the Bible's story of the Code of Hammurabi—if one is wronged, it meant an eye for an eye in retribution. It was a black-and-white world where mental illness wasn't recognized as a "real thing," and there was no gray area, no nuances to be considered when there was a crime committed against one of their own.

After Vicky's stroke in 2012, I became well acquainted with the Puxico Police Department, which consisted of an elected City Marshal, eight officers, and two drug dogs (one trained by the City Marshal himself). I was a former chief of police for a small agency and now teaching criminal justice, and I felt comfortable talking to the Puxico officers. The City Marshal, Johnny Clark, and his officers were frequently called to Vicky and Chris' trailer home. And as their drug use increased, so did the violence. I received so many terrifying calls from Vicky. The police department was also getting emergency calls from Vicky in addition to the times I called requesting they check on Vicky's welfare. The calls increased in frequency and became progressively disturbing.

In March 2012 Vicky called begging for me to save her from Chris. "Sissy, please help me," she pleaded over the phone as she locked herself in the bathroom. In the background, I could hear Chris bang on the door, yelling "I'm going to kill you for takin' my pills." During another call, Vicky told me that Chris had punched her in the chest, where only days earlier a heart stent had been placed. Another time she called me because Chris barricaded himself in their trailer with Mom's old .22 handgun and a couple of shotguns, then locked all the doors and windows. Once again, I frantically made a call to the Puxico Police Department.

While locked inside, Chris repeated one of his favorite threats: to kill Vicky's beloved dog, Snowball. "Go out there and make sure they don't arrest me, or I'm going to slit that dog's throat and yours next."

When the officer returned with a search warrant, Vicky pleaded with the officer not to arrest Chris. He didn't budge and held off the officers for a few hours until they could coax him into unlocking the doors and putting the weapons away. There was no arrest made that night, nor was he arrested after any of these incidents. When I later asked Chris about these violent episodes, he would say Vicky was making it up, or he got angry, calling me profane names and hanging up the phone.

37

When I asked the Puxico police why no one got arrested, they said they were using officer discretion. Since 1989, Missouri law allows officers to use personal discretion on domestic violence calls. An officer isn't obligated to arrest the alleged primary aggressor but must file a report if no arrest is made. Suppose an officer responds to the same address within 12 hours with a similar circumstance of domestic violence. In that case, it is mandatory to establish a primary aggressor, and an arrest must be made. Often, rural police departments know the residents when they are sent on calls. They can be neighbors and the people they see every Sunday at church. Officers don't want to rock the boat, or worse. More commonly, they don't understand the dynamics of domestic violence, and dismiss physical assault incidents within a family as normal behavior.

𝕴 was conflicted between my police instincts and experience, and my unquestioning love for my sister. Vicky, with her history of mental illness, traumatic brain injury, and drug abuse, was married to an equally damaged person. Was it plausible that she killed her husband? Kenny was on record as threatening and assaulting Vicky during the few weeks he lived with them. Was her confession a hallucination or something more? Was it a guilty mother's attempt to sacrifice herself for her son?

A criminal investigator relies on her well-honed instincts, but how could I compartmentalize my fierce need to protect Vicky? I didn't know if I could set all that aside to look at the facts and analyze witness statements objectively. But one thing I did know: She needed a lawyer. The Missouri Public Defender system is like every other in the country—overworked and under-budgeted. The first call I made was to the best criminal defense attorney in St. Louis, Missouri, who had successfully won a case against Stoddard County involving a 13-year-old boy who was arrested and charged with the murder of his 64-year-old neighbor. I heard a speech this attorney gave on the death penalty at a local synagogue, and his message of compassion had stayed with me. I made an appointment for later in the afternoon at his office in Clayton, Missouri.

All day long, I gathered as much information about the case as I could to prepare for my appointment with the renowned defense attorney. When I arrived at his office and saw the opulent decor, I was reminded that his services were far beyond our price range. In the speech I heard, he spoke with such understanding about the defendants in the murder cases he won that I thought it would not hurt to plead Vicky's case and explain all the challenges in the hope he might take the case at a reduced fee. He recognized me from our previous brief meeting, and took me back to his office and sat in front of me, his lips pursed, listening to my tale of domestic violence, prescription drug abuse, and the horror that is life in Stoddard County. After hearing my story, he advised me of the price of hiring an expert like him.

"Well, it would be $75,000 to retain me to start the case. What is your husband's and your occupation?"

"I am an adjunct professor, and my husband does maintenance."

"Do you have any land, a car, or a house you can put up as collateral?"

"No. Not really."

"To be honest with you, you can't afford me."

He was right. One couch in his waiting room costs more than all the furniture in my house. There was no way we could afford him. I had hoped he would have found the same compassion for Vicky that he so eloquently spoke of when he defended other indigent murder suspects. I wasn't looking for free work, just a lawyer to have mercy on my brain-damaged, drug-addicted sister who only had a ninth-grade education.

I walked out of the office, defeated just like I had been when I first heard the news of Vicky's arrest. I doubted if she could get a fair trial. Chris' large extended family were lifelong residents of Puxico and the greater Stoddard County area, which produced many votes for the elected officials, including the Marshal, Sheriff,

39

Prosecutor, and Judges. Vicky was a nobody with no voice and no chance for mercy.

We are not wealthy people. I couldn't drop my work commitments at the St. Louis area universities where I teach criminal justice. I didn't make it down to Stoddard County to see Vicky in jail until a few weeks after her arrest. I was still unsure if I even wanted to see her. Instead of fighting that internal battle with myself, I distracted my racing brain by diving into work: taking extra time to grade class assignments, researching new curricula, and even cleaning our stove—anything to think about, something other than Vicky. I couldn't sleep for more than a few hours at a time. Food didn't taste right. I was still in shock and trying to process what happened.

I couldn't even talk to Vicky because the method to contact inmates was so convoluted. First, the jail only allowed outbound calls. But Vicky struggled to remember her own phone number, let alone mine. If I wanted to see her in person, she had to remember to add me to her visitors list and then have me approved by the jail prior to visiting.

I cautiously spoke to Kenny over those weeks immediately after Vicky's arrest. I hoped to find more or new information to clarify who was really responsible for Chris' death. Kenny called me every day but only talked about Mom or old memories for hours and occasionally about the murder. I am an experienced detective who specialized in investigating sex crimes, which required patience and skill in listening and empathy; the first and best technique I learned was to bottle your emotions and let a suspect talk. Kenny was the only other person who could tell the true story of what happened that day. I would sit back and wait for the truth... if it would ever come.

Chris' funeral was a few days after his death. Kenny insisted on paying his respects. I found it odd that Kenny wanted to attend the funeral. I told Kenny it wasn't a good idea, but he went anyway. Our older sister Trixie sent flowers. It seemed an odd gesture;

I don't know if I would have wanted flowers from my brother's murderer's family.

Kenny was still living at the trailer and Chris' family had been coming by and asking to take things. Kenny didn't know what to do because they weren't his belongings to give away, nor did he want to antagonize the Isaac family in their grief. He told them to come back later. I reminded him that some of the property was Vicky's, and as awful as the situation was, it wasn't up to him, or the Isaacs, to decide who gets what; the courts would decide.

By the end of May, I had a few days off from work and drove with my teenage son Julian from St. Louis to Puxico to see Kenny. Kenny had no means to support himself while waiting for his Social Security benefits to begin. My sister Trixie and I sent him a little money, but the immediate issue was that the air conditioner no longer worked in the trailer. With its small windows and metal sides, a mobile home's design acts as an oven during the heat and humidity of a Missouri summer and can be deadly. If the outside temperatures are in the 90s, the inside temperature is well over 100 degrees. Kenny had been sleeping outside until the mosquito-laden night air drove him back inside. Installing a new air conditioner was a priority.

During the three-hour drive, my mind played tug of war. I told myself the only reason for coming down was to give Kenny some relief from the heat, not for me to start an investigation. But the detective in me could not be denied. I kept turning the events over in my head. Given Vicky's current mental state and abusive, chaotic home life, maybe she thought killing Chris was her only way out. Yet I had a nagging doubt about Kenny's involvement, and different scenarios played in my mind as the yellow lines of the highway passed by.

The first thing I noticed when we arrived was that Vicky's dog, Snowball, was gone. The dog was a beautiful pit bull/Shar-Pei mix who lived in a doghouse near the front porch. Her doghouse was empty, and her water dish was overturned. Vicky loved the dog so much that she had Snowball's picture and name tattooed on her left

41

shoulder. I used to poke fun about the tattoo, but when Chris had threatened to kill the dog, I understood why Vicky had Snowball's image indelibly marked on her skin and with her forever.

The trailer—the home she loved—appeared abandoned. The surrounding grass was higher than usual. The vehicles were gone. The cars were registered in both her and Chris' names, and even with Chris dead, they still belonged to Vicky. Later, I found out that while Vicky and Kenny were interrogated, the Stoddard County Sheriff's Department allowed Chris' family to come inside the trailer—an active crime scene—and remove household items and the cars.

Kenny met us at the end of the driveway, smiling, wearing blue jeans and a long-sleeved T-shirt. It was at least 85 degrees, and with the humidity, it felt more like 100 degrees. He never had much fashion sense. Walmart or yard sale clothes were good enough for him. Still, he wore blue jeans and was fully covered in the dripping heat. I examined him, sizing up his facial expressions for guilt or innocence. As I stopped the car, he leaned into the window.

"You don't want to go into that house. It is hot as hell. I saw the devil in the corner, and he told me 'forget this, I am going back to hell to cool off.'" He laughed.

"Where is Snowball?" I asked.

"I gave her and Biscuit to the Isaacs," Kenny said.

"What? Vicky loves those dogs," I said.

"Well, I can't look after them," Kenny replied.

Kenny never had the patience for animals and didn't want the responsibility of Vicky's dogs. He gave Snowball and her other dog, a small Chihuahua, Biscuit, to people who hated her. Visions of Snowball being used as a bait dog in a fighting ring filled my head. He knew how much those dogs meant to Vicky. I forced down my rising anger and focused on the task at hand.

"Well, I have to measure the window for you so I can put in the air conditioner," I said, putting the car into park. I would have rather been in a gang shootout than go into that house. Kenny opened the back door that led into the kitchen. The heat and stench took my breath away. It was like putting your head into a 450-degree oven.

"I told you it was hot," Kenny said.

"No, it is not hot. It's fuckin' awful," I said.

The trailer was a three-bedroom, two-bathroom model. Mobile homes have a standard layout of the kitchen and living room as the main rooms, then a long hallway that leads to a bathroom and bedrooms. On the left was the kitchen, the right the living room, and against the wall was an obviously bloodstained couch.

I started recreating the crime scene in my head as I walked through. Chris must have been shot while lying on his right side because of the elongated pools of uneven red lines running from the top to the bottom of the couch.

"Why is this still here?" I asked, pointing to the blood-soaked sofa.

"What am I gonna do with it? I cleaned up underneath it. The Sheriff's Department gave me some gloves. Chris' dad and brother Elmer said they wanted to take the couch," Kenny said, pulling out a box of disposable gloves from one of the kitchen cabinets. He held the box of gloves in front of my face for an extended amount of time. The brand, Mr. Clean, was a cheap household kind and not a brand or type that a law enforcement agency would purchase.

"What?" I said, surprised at his comment. "What the hell are the Isaacs gonna do with this couch?"

"I don't know. They are gonna put it in someone's house," Kenny replied, putting the gloves finally back into the cabinet.

"It should be burned," my son Julian chimed in.

Julian moved the first cushion, and we all jumped back in revulsion; there was a clump of brain matter wedged between the armrest and covered spring section of the couch.

"You were interrogated for half the day, then they brought you back here to the crime scene with blood and brains fermenting in the heat and humidity and told you to clean it up yourself?"

"Yeah. This ain't St. Louis. They don't have a crime scene clean-up unit."

The humane thing would be to have someone trained and ready for these types of situations. Even if there weren't many homicides in this area, somebody somewhere in that county

43

would like an opportunity to make some extra money for when that service is needed. Or, at the very least, connect Kenny with a charity or church group that would volunteer to help clean as an act of mercy and mission.

I turned to the task at hand, measuring the window. I asked Kenny if he had a fan. The sweat was pooling on my forehead and dripping from my face.

"If I can find one. I have one in the back bedroom, but it is under a bunch of stuff."

I walked back to the bedroom with him to try to get some air going through the house. The entire trailer, from the hallway, the middle bedroom, to the back bedroom, was filled top to bottom with junk. The middle bedroom was crammed floor to ceiling with cheap, framed paintings. I couldn't even walk inside the room. The back bedroom, where Kenny slept, was filled with dolls—over two hundred Cabbage Patch Kids, Beanie Babies, porcelain and rag dolls. Although having a doll collection was a family tradition that began with my grandmother, no one had hundreds of dolls. The shelves were crammed tight with brass knick-knacks. There was just enough room for Kenny to sleep on the bed. We walked back to the largest bedroom, where Vicky and Chris slept, located on the other end of the trailer. DVDs, clothes, and NASCAR memorabilia filled the room. The bathroom had dried shit on the toilet bowl and spread across the surrounding walls. The pungent smell of urine from the unflushed toilet bowl filled the air. The shower had a thick ring of black filth around it.

"Who smeared shit on the walls?" I asked.

"Oh, Chris would have accidents when he was on his pills. And I guess they didn't have toilet paper sometimes," Kenny answered, trying to downplay the disgusting conditions and come up with some explanation.

I quickly shut the door of the bathroom.

At that moment, I realized why I wasn't allowed in Vicky's house for the past two years. She said it was because Chris didn't like me, but I think the truth was she was embarrassed by the wretched state of the house. Mom instilled obsessive housekeeping skills in her children, and I knew that Vicky used to keep a clean house. The hoarding must have been caused by a soul-destroying mix of pills, mental illness, abuse, and isolation.

As we walked out, I saw an open journal filled with Vicky's handwriting beside the bed. It was how she kept track of her bills and how she planned how to use their Social Security benefits. (The list-making and daydreaming of how to spend money was another habit she picked up from our Mom.) There were also diary-like notes from the last few months.

March 20th - *"Stop eating so much and go outside."*

March 28th - *"I hate myself. I wish death would come for me."*

March 29th - *"Had a better day. Played with Snowball and Biscuit."*

April 3rd - *"Paid bills. Didn't eat much. Good day."*

April 17th - *"I would be better off dead. I made my bed. I have to lie in it."*

The journal painted a picture of her lonely struggles but didn't sound suicidal. It sounded like she had resigned herself to her fate, again accepting blame for being a victim of abuse.

Julian and I wanted out of that house. I quickly measured the grim, crusted window. With no department stores in Puxico, we drove the 25 miles to a store in Poplar Bluff to buy an air conditioner.

Poplar Bluff was a stark contrast to Puxico. Decades ago, it had been the main stop for the railroad between Memphis and St. Louis. The city boasts a population of 17,000, dotted with modest houses, hospitals, restaurants, and stores. The Black River meanders through the east and south side of the town. Three Rivers Community College and other technical schools provide a way out of a dead-end life if you decide to pursue the educational opportunity. Poplar Bluff had a magic about it. It was a small town, but anything seemed possible, yet I dreamed of leaving it my whole life. Still, Poplar Bluff didn't have the overwhelming and pervasive sense of desperation and loneliness of Puxico.

We found a reasonably priced air conditioner, ate some pizza, and went back to Puxico. On the drive, I asked Kenny more about the day of the murder, but I had to tread lightly so as not to raise suspicion.

"Do you want me to contact Missouri Crime Victims Compensation to get you some counseling?"

"Ol' Firewood is okay. Sometimes I just need a little time in the hospital."

"Yeah, what happened when the police took you to the hospital a few weeks ago?"

"Well, living with them was making me nervous, and I just needed a break from that trailer."

"What did the doctors say?"

"They said I have Narcissistic Personality Disorder. You know, like Narcissus from Greek mythology. He looked at his reflection in a pool of water and fell in love with it. You know."

"Is that all they said?" I dug a little further.

"Well, you know the doctoring profession, they want to make up stuff all the time. Why do you think they call it practicing medicine? They ain't good at it yet. They said I had the old schizophrenia. Ain't that something? They don't know."

I could understand Narcissistic Personality Disorder diagnosis, but his blasé declaration that he had schizophrenia shocked me. For years we thought Kenny's behavior was a combination of eccentricity and alcohol abuse.

"Kenny, are you taking medicine for your schizophrenia?" I asked.

"I am now. But that's just something they just said I have. Same thing the doctors told me back after Grandma died. I take their little medicine for a while and make myself better."

Twelve years! Mom died over a decade ago and this was the first time I heard that Kenny had a diagnosis of schizophrenia. He never told me because he didn't believe it to be true. I wondered if Vicky knew. I was reminded of the probable cause statement of how "voices told her to end him." It was more plausible that Kenny heard the voices telling *him* to kill and not Vicky.

46

I wanted to talk more about his diagnosis, but he seemed uncomfortable to continue the conversation once schizophrenia was mentioned. Television shows often portray police interviews as an officer pointing an accusatory finger in the suspect's face. That's not how it happens at all. A good interrogator finds common ground with the suspect, befriends them, and gains their trust. There was a chance he might not ever tell the truth of what happened that May morning. His having schizophrenia didn't change my thoughts about his guilt as it seemed more likely than ever before that Kenny's mental illness combined with Vicky and Chris' drug usage and instability in that pressure cooker of a trailer escalated into violence.

Once we arrived back at the trailer, I helped Kenny install the new air conditioner in the living room window only a few feet from the blood-streaked couch. I asked Kenny if he wanted to stay with us at the hotel.

"No. I'm fine right here. It will get cooled off. I hope Satan don't come back. I'll have to turn it off," he joked.

Even with all my lingering uncertainty, Julian and I didn't want to leave him in the sadness and filth of the trailer, but he refused to come with us.

I had so many doubts about what was written in the official police reports versus what really happened on that May morning. Kenny made such a point to show me the box of disposable gloves. I couldn't get it out of my mind that a Sheriff's Department would give their deputies such cheap, low-quality, dollar-store gloves. As small and underfunded as Stoddard County was, the liability issue of exposing an officer to harm from handling lethal fentanyl or contaminating a crime scene would outweigh the cost of buying better gloves.

That night at the hotel, after a long week of this hellish nightmare begun by that late-night phone call, I fell asleep and dreamed of a moment from my childhood. In the dream, ten-year-old Vicky and six-year-old me lay on our childhood bed together. We whispered in the dark about her dog, Carriebeth, a white Chihuahua mix who was the mother of my dog, Max.

Animals always made Vicky happy. The sticky Missouri humidity caused beads of sweat to roll down our faces. Our trailer's tin sides and the wood paneling kept the heat inside. There was slight relief from the rotating window fan. I didn't care that my uneven, home-haircut bangs stuck to my forehead. I enjoyed this time with her. Lights from a car outside illuminated her chubby cherub cheeks and perfectly natural straight teeth as she smiled and told a story about what a good mother Carriebeth was to her puppies. The car stopped.

"It's Mom," she said.

We never knew which Mom would emerge from that car—the Mom who brought us cold hamburgers and fries from the Broadway Café and told us stories of her night or the Mom who stumbled in drunk and let the littlest things make her angry.

The door flung open.

"Kids!" Mom yelled. "Where the hell you at?"

A crash of a body hitting the worn linoleum kitchen floor scared us.

"Who the hell put this doll here? Where the hell are you fuckin' kids?"

I held my Whoopsie doll as tight as I could, wishing in some way she could tell my mom to go to sleep. As her footsteps got louder and closer, my tiny legs started shaking. Vicky's face looked as if she was steeling herself for the coming onslaught. There was a storm coming, and we knew it was a storm of fists.

"You fuckin' kids don't clean up nothing," she said, slamming the door against the wall. She grabbed my left arm and pulled me out of bed.

"How many goddamn times do I have to tell you about picking your shit up? What is it going to take to get it through your thick fuckin' skull?"

She threw me onto the floor and took off her shoe. I braced my doll and awaited her shoe heel to smack my back.

Vicky jumped up and said, "Stop, stop. I left the doll there."

Mom pushed her back onto the bed. Another hit of her heel landed in the middle of my back. Vicky jumped in front of the next swing.

"You want some of it too?" Mom said. She pulled Vicky by the hair off the bed and kicked her into the hallway. As I lay on the floor, a crumpled mess, white-knuckling Whoopsie, the fight continued in the hallway and front room.

"Go ahead. Hit me. Go ahead and hit me," Vicky screamed.

The smacks continued, and I lost count after ten. I sat up, crying with my fingers in my ears. I couldn't take the sounds of the hitting. A few minutes later, I heard my mom yelling, "Get your ass to bed."

Vicky returned to bed, her mouth and face covered in blood. Her legs were beginning to bruise as more blood from the newly inflicted kicks and wallops began to flow.

I swiped my eyes and got back into bed with her. "Why did you do that?"

Vicky wiped the blood from the corner of her mouth and fell onto the bed.

"I don't know. I am hard-headed. I can take it. I probably deserve it."

No, she didn't deserve to be thrown like a rag doll and beaten like a dirty old rug. Neither did she deserve to be sitting in a jail cell—a psychiatric institution maybe, but not a prison for the rest of her life. As I lay there, remembering how she defended me from the worst of Mom's beatings, I knew I had to help her. It was my turn to protect Vicky from her latest abuser—the Missouri criminal justice system.

Mom and Grandpa Eugene, Poplar Bluff, Missouri 1935

CHAPTER TWO

I couldn't stop thinking of Mom. How did our family get so messed up? Why was I missing her? Of course, I was relieved that she wasn't here to see the trouble Vicky was in, but I could've used her whirlwind of anger to get to the truth and protect her family. I'd like to think she would have fought *for* Vicky in this situation. I know she would have never wanted Kenny to be stuck in that trailer wrestling with a disease that he wouldn't acknowledge. Mom controlled their lives so completely that Vicky and Kenny both fell apart when she died.

Mom didn't have much formal education, but she more than made up for it with a canny fighter's intelligence. She reminded me of the yellow poplar trees that lined the bluffs of Black River and gave my hometown its name—tall, stately, and full of flowering beauty. At 5'7", her temper was fiery as her red hair, and her emerald-green eyes hid years of disappointment and pain. I kept thinking back about all the incidents, all the tragedies, and all the violence that shaped how our family became so dysfunctional.

Mom started life on December 15, 1932, during the lowest point of the Great Depression, in a dirt-floor log cabin without indoor plumbing or electricity, set back in the woods of rural Poplar Bluff, Missouri. Mom's parents were Grandpa Eugene, a kind-hearted alcoholic, and callous Grandma Roxie, who carried the Frizzell propensity for violence and kept the family under her thumb. It wasn't a kind or loving home. Mom would often tell me, "No one has told me what to do since I was eleven years old."

In 1943, Eugene got a job working on the Tennessee Valley Pipeline, and every week the family rode the ten miles to Poplar Bluff in a horse-drawn wagon to see Eugene leave with the work crews as they traveled throughout Arkansas and further south to lay pipe. On the monthly payday Friday, Roxie took Mom back to Poplar Bluff as they scoured the taverns on both sides of the train tracks to look for Eugene, who was prone to drinking his paycheck. Roxie was of the only-for-appearances kind of Christian and refused to be seen going into the bars, but she had no qualms sending Mom into them to retrieve Eugene and his money. Mom had to find him before the bar whores or hustlers stole all his cash, or else the family didn't eat.

Mom found Eugene passed out at the bar. The bartender knew Mom by name because this wasn't the first time she had pulled her father out of a bar. He told her a rather large, redheaded barfly just took all of Eugene's money and was hiding out in the toilet. The barfly went to a private stall to count her takings lifted from Eugene's pocket. Mom walked into the bathroom and spotted her counting money and smiling from ear to ear. Always a scrappy fighter, she scanned the room and planned how an eleven-year-old girl could fight a full-grown woman. Mom went into the stall and unscrewed the toilet seat with a barrette from her hair. She used the toilet seat lid to beat the woman into unconsciousness with her little hands. Mom didn't escape unscathed. The barfly managed to tear the earring out of Mom's right earlobe before going to the ground in defeat. Mom and the bartender carried Eugene outside to Roxie and into the wagon, and they got him home. Mom later learned that the barfly almost died and ended up with permanent brain damage. Mom's earlobe was damaged beyond repair. Every time I looked at Mom's scarred ear, I saw her lost childhood.

Mom's answer to every problem was fighting. I watched Mom attack a lot of people throughout my childhood for what she assumed was disrespect toward her. When I was about five years old, while we were shopping at a department store, we ran into a local liquor store owner. Mom placed me in a shopping cart beside her car and said to me, "Don't move."

The lady had sold my brother alcohol, allowed him to leave the store, then called the police. He was pulled over and arrested for a minor in possession of alcohol charge. Mom went up to the woman as she walked to her car and asked her, "Why did you set up my son?"

The lady mumbled something.

"What did you say?" Mom asked her. The lady kept walking. "Heh, bitch, you got something to say to me?"

The lady turned and yelled, "He shouldn't have been buying alcohol."

Mom grabbed the woman and swung her around. Mom punched her in the face, and blood flew out of her nose. The woman fell back on the hood of her car. I put my fingers in my ears and covered my eyes with my hand. I looked out between the spaces of my fingers. Mom punched her repeatedly in the face and head. The woman tried to get away, but Mom grabbed her arm and threw her against the car. Finally, employees came out to stop the fight, but Mom was done.

"Teach you next time, you law-calling bitch," Mom said. After ending up with a broken arm and two black eyes, neither the lady nor the store employees called the police.

When I was suspended the last three days of my sophomore year of high school for fighting during an assembly, the principal called Mom to the school. I was terrified as the principal told her about the fight and suspension. Mom asked me what started the fight. I told her a girl pulled my hair. The principal asked Mom what she was going to do about it.

"Well, did you win?" Mom asked me.

"Yeah, I think so," I responded.

"Mrs. Pickard, the girl might have a concussion. What are you going to do with your daughter?" The principal asked.

"She won. What the hell do you want me to do? I am gonna take her to Frosty to get something to eat. Betty, get your stuff."

We left, and Mom didn't say anything else about the fight, but she looked at me with pride for the next few weeks.

I loved watching *Wonder Woman* on television as a girl. It was my Halloween costume for five years straight. I wanted her golden lasso because it made people tell the truth, and I needed the truth because it wasn't told in my house. Wonder Woman was strong, beautiful, and intelligent—the qualities I admired in Mom at that young age. I related to Wonder Woman's Amazonian ways because those were the qualities Mom wanted for us: to be smart and educated, not to be dependent on anyone but yourself, and never back away from a fight.

For my first eight years of life, our home was a mobile home outside Poplar Bluff's city limits. Our trailer was on ten acres and was as secluded as the comic book land of Wonder Woman's Themyscira. I pretended we were our own tribe of Amazonians— five females living self-sufficiently in a heavily wooded area. Mom was Queen Hippolyta, who taught her daughters to live off the land. In the summer, we planted a large garden and picked wild blackberries from the side of the road, canning whatever vegetables and fruits were left over. There were two ponds filled with fish to catch. We helped Mom clean the butchered chickens and field dress the deer and turkeys she shot. We carried rusty well water to the animals and chopped firewood for heat in the winter. Mom worked on her own cars—she could do everything from changing the oil to swapping out a transmission.

Mom believed that men were the weaker sex. She understood that men controlled her world, but she viewed them as stupid and weak. There were very few men worthy of love and appreciation. She was attracted to intense men. She had tattoos at a time when only criminals, outlaws, and circus folk had them. Her tattoos gave clues to the men who were in her love life. On her hands, she wore the tattoos made famous by Robert Mitchum in the 1955 movie *Night of the Hunter*, the word "LOVE" on the knuckles of her right hand and "HATE" on the left. As she told us, she would love you with one hand and hate you with the other. On her right arm was the word "Slick," and her left arm bore the initials "DWT," both indelibly inked forever in a hasty show of loyalty. These tattoos served as a tribute to two men who were career criminals and convicted murderers. "Slick" led one of the worst prison riots in Missouri Penitentiary history. "DWT" was an escaped inmate who went on a killing crime spree. I remember answering collect calls from the Missouri Penitentiary system, but by the time I was in fourth grade, there were no more phone calls. No more killers.

Later, she began to date another type of man: musicians who allowed her a temporary escape from the harsh reality of being a low-income single mom. She would go to the bars and clubs to hear her current boyfriends play. Mom never had trouble attracting

Mom with car, Poplar Bluff, Missouri 1955

the opposite sex and was a consummate flirt who could charm anyone when she chose. Of the five different men who fathered all eight of us, three were married to other people at the time of our respective conceptions. She had other relationships besides ones that produced children. However, when she did marry and wanted to leave, she just left, never bothering to get a divorce. The law and government institutions were things to be avoided.

Love was never kind to Mom. Her first taste of it was at age 18 when she met a handsome sailor named Johnny Shrum. In his tailored Navy uniform, there must have been something special because he stole her heart, and after a quick courtship, they conceived my oldest sister Jackie in 1950. Their love was all-consuming, but like everything else in Mom's life, anything good was repaid a hundredfold in heartache. Johnny was killed in a tragic car wreck in Washington state when Jackie was nine months old. I don't think Mom ever recovered from his death. She shut down emotionally and never gave her heart completely to a man again. She would tell me, *"They can't break what they don't have."*

A few years later, she met John Hurley. Another John, but that was where the similarities ended. He was far from the love of her life. He was a much older, successful business owner. In fact, he had children nearly the same age as Mom. He fathered four of my siblings. One of the boys, Geno, died as a toddler, and a daughter named Victoria (before Vicky's birth) was stillborn. Not long after that, John himself died of heart failure.

In, 1961, Mom met Aubrey. He was driving a tow truck for a friend when he saw the statuesque, red-haired stunner that was my mother on the side of the road with a flat tire. Soon, they welcomed their only biological child, my sister Trixie, in 1962. He, like John Hurley, was much older than Mom. Maybe she was too scared to love someone that she could grow old with because, in her life, love doesn't grow old. Although Aubrey would never take the place of Johnny Shrum, he did love my mother. He would pamper her by giving her foot massages. He was a good father that would bring home little surprises for us kids. Maybe Mom thought she had finally cheated heartache. She was wrong. She would have two more children, Vicky and me, by other men, before Aubrey was struck by a drunk driver and left with brain damage then dying a short time later in 1976.

Mom's love life was murky during the time Vicky was conceived in February 1965. No one has any idea of the identity of Vicky's father. We suspected it was a man named Charles, an alcoholic who died working on a riverboat. Even though Mom had already given the name Victoria to her stillborn child, she used it again because the name has been a tradition for generations in Mom's family, and she wanted a child to have the name. To forestall any confusion, my living sister is called Vicky. My father, I would later learn, was a married man from the other side of town. I met him and his parents a few times, but mostly Mom and I had to sneak around to meet him. To me, he was just some random man who gave us money.

All these memories flooded my overtired brain day after day. I needed to see Vicky and find out for myself, from her, what happened that day in May at her trailer.

It is an arduous process to speak to an incarcerated person—the jail contracts out phone services with different companies. An inmate gets a few free minutes to contact someone. If a person wants to communicate with the inmate, they must set up an account with the private company. The jails and prisons receive a portion of the call revenue. It is more expensive to call an inmate from the same state than to make an international call.

I needed to speak to Vicky no matter what the cost. However, I knew she didn't remember my phone number. The only way to get through to her was to send a letter with my phone number and wait for her to call. It took three days for the letter to arrive at the jail, then another day for it to get sorted and handed out. Ten days later, my phone rang, and a recorded message said, "This is a collect call from [a recording of Vicky saying her name] an inmate at the Stoddard County Jail. To accept charges, press 1."

I pressed "1" as fast as my fingers could.

"Sis, are you there?" Vicky said.

"Yes, what is going on?" I said, relieved to hear her voice.

"Not much. I'm in jail. But I can't figure out why Kenny and Chris have not come to get me. I've been waiting," she said.

"Do you know why you're there?"

"No. I guess I had got a DUI and had a car wreck. Nobody will tell me anything."

"Vicky, you are charged with murdering Chris."

"What? I killed Chris in the car wreck? What about Kenny? Please say I didn't hurt my boy?"

"No, they are saying you shot Chris in the head with Mom's old .22. Kenny is okay. He's staying at the trailer."

"I couldn't have done that. That must be the picture I got in the mail. But it must be a car wreck."

"What picture?"

"The picture Chris' sister Doris sent me of Chris covered in blood. I thought it was a joke. I just threw it in the trash."

Vicky seemed disoriented, and her speech was slow, like she was unsure how to talk and struggled to put words together. I worried that this was the start of a stroke.

"Are you taking your blood pressure medicine?"

"Yes, but I feel light-headed."

"Okay, we don't have much time. I will call the jail, and you put me on your visitors list. I will be down there next Saturday." A month had passed since her arrest. I needed to see her, talk to her in person—or what was left of her.

"Okay."

There were little to no mental health resources available to her while in county jail. I couldn't imagine waking up in jail and not knowing where I was or the reason for being there. This was not the conversation I wanted to have, and all my questions about Kenny's schizophrenia would have to wait for another day.

I couldn't understand why anyone would mail Vicky an autopsy photo or how the jail staff allowed it to be given to Vicky, who obviously didn't even know why she was in jail. For someone to take the time to send a bloody picture of Chris on the autopsy table is not revenge—it is just cruel. Not only to Vicky but to Chris. How disrespectful to his memory to get a jab in on Vicky, who didn't even know what she was looking at.

I called the jail to speak to the jail administrator. I needed to find out if Vicky was getting the correct medicine and dosage, especially her blood pressure medicine.

"Jail Administrator," a male voice answered.

"Yes, this is Betty Frizzell calling about Victoria Isaac."

"Let me see. Isaac, you say? Hold on, darling, let me look," he said.

The rest of the call consisted of him calling me "sweetie" and "honey." I was polite and held my tongue and eventually found out that Vicky was *not* getting her correct meds.

I detested being called "darling" by anyone but my family. I overlooked it because, in southeast Missouri, men used diminutive endearments as part of the culture that long suppressed women, and I needed to make sure that Vicky got what she needed before seeing that they treated me with respect. (Years later, this very same jail administrator would be convicted and imprisoned for rape.)

I hung up the phone with the familiar feelings of dismissal I experienced as a female officer. Mom had prepared me for this battle since birth. *"Men hold all the control in this world. You are gonna hafta work twice as hard as them. They will try to break you. Don't you let them... The only weapon you got is you. Make them work for your respect."*

I lived by those words when I started my law enforcement career about 30 miles from Poplar Bluff, as a Deputy Sheriff, with the Ripley County Sheriff's Department. I was the only female the department, hired a few days before graduating from the academy. As a rookie, I solved a string of burglaries in the south part of the county. The story attracted press, and after a big write-up in the local newspaper, people, men particularly, called me the "little girl deputy." Later, when I became a detective working for the Lincoln County Sheriff's office, some of my male co-workers said

I was given the position because the department had to promote a woman. When I booked in two suspects whom I tracked for 24 hours straight, who used stolen automobiles to smash into businesses and steal safes and ATM machines in a two-county crime spree, I heard my co-worker say, "Betty was only made a detective because they needed a token female." I turned to him and said, "Being a woman may have helped me get hired but being good has kept me here."

Before I retired to teach criminal forensics and policing techniques, I was one of only three female chiefs of police in the entire state of Missouri. And still, I would answer the phone, and the caller would ask to speak to the Chief, not his secretary. The jail administrator in Stoddard County wasn't the first to use my gender as a reason to dismiss me—just the latest.

The next day Kenny called to tell me that Vicky needed to have someone appointed as Power of Attorney. I was surprised to find out that the jail allowed Kenny to visit Vicky as he was the only witness in her murder case. The prosecutors I worked with throughout my career would have never let a witness visit a suspect. Kenny's testimony and her confession were the key pieces of evidence critical to the murder case. Allowing them to have conversations could jeopardize the prosecution's case.

"I told her if you want to keep your stuff and help your case, you better sign those papers once Aunt Betty gets them fixed up," Kenny said.

"Kenny, it is the weekend. I have to wait until Monday to hire an attorney," I replied.

"She also put you on her visitors list. You can go see her next week."

"Okay. Julian and I will be down next week," I informed Kenny.

On that Friday, Kenny called to tell me that Chris' brother Elmer (the "nice one" that had impressed Mom) had been to the house asking why I was getting the Power of Attorney paperwork.

Elmer said the attorney I retained called him and told him what I was doing. The attorney told Elmer he would stall the paperwork until Chris' family filed probate court paperwork. I called the attorney's office, but he was unavailable.

"Is the paperwork done?" I asked his secretary.

"Oh, yes, Mrs. Frizzell," she said.

"I will be there tomorrow to pick it up. And tell him I will be filing a complaint with the Missouri Bar Association."

Less than an hour later, Vicky called. She had the paperwork from the attorney. One of my fears for Vicky was coming true: that small-town politics and friendships with the Isaac family would hurt Vicky in getting the help she needed, which would have also been the justice Chris deserved. If my hunch was right, it was Kenny and not Vicky who killed Chris.

Driving down to the jail, I thought about a younger Vicky when she was the chubby troublemaker who played with animals and had an intense devotion to our abusive mother. I thought about the times after she moved home with toddler-aged Kenny, still young and beautiful, listening to Fleetwood Mac. When Mom was mad at us, we would cruise around Poplar Bluff in her van for hours listening to music and talking. Now I visited her in a jail cell.

The Stoddard County Jail is an older building from the early 1980s with dark brown brick on the bottom and tiny bubble-glass windows on the top. The windows allow light in, but those on the inside can't see out—like a tease for the beauty from the outside. The jail reception area looks like a throwback from Stalin-era Russia, dark gray with a matching gray metal desk, and cold. The waiting room was filled with hard plastic chairs.

"Can I see your driver's license or identification?" he asked, not even looking at me.

"Yes," I said, handing it to him.

"Betty Frizzell," he said, looking at my identification.

"Yes."

"Who are you here to see?" he inquired while typing in my information, looking for warrants.

"My sister, Victoria Isaac."

He looked at me. "Oh, you are that Betty Frizzell. Have a seat. She will be down in about five minutes."

"Do you know me?"

"No, Mrs. Frizzell. Just heard about you."

"What did you hear?"

"Nothing. Please have a seat." He smiled and handed back my license.

A little confused, I took a seat. A few seconds later, I saw a man behind the glass standing next to the correctional officer talking and pointing at me. I waved and smiled as if to say *I see you like you see me*. The man and the correctional officer quickly turned. I thought about Mom's advice: show no fear.

Another correctional officer came out and yelled, "Those seeing prisoner Isaac go to the window."

The booth was just a phone, a glass window with another phone, and a tiny stainless-steel stool bolted to the ground. My heart started to pound with anticipation. As the door opened, I could see Vicky, wearing an orange jumpsuit. All 5'6" of her looked so much older; gone was the bleached blonde, replaced by longer graying hair, yet she was smiling for the first time in years, it seemed. She almost skipped to the phone.

"Heh, sis. Whatcha doing?" she asked with a smile.

I was disheartened to see how happy someone facing life in prison could be. Her life on the outside must have been much worse.

"I am doing good. How about you?"

"I'm fine," she replied.

Then I noticed one of her teeth was missing. "Where is your partial tooth?"

"They won't let me have it because they're worried I will shank someone."

I started to swell up with tears and anger. "What? That is fuckin' ridiculous and inhumane. Do you want me to call up here and raise hell?"

"No. They told me you called."

"They don't need to worry about me because I will call and call."

"I'm all right, sis. I might lose weight in here."

Abused children always find a bright spot in the worst of circumstances. As she was trying to make me feel better, her facial expressions were the same as the little girl who fought so bravely to defend me against Mom's beatings. I couldn't stop the tears. I had to stop crying but couldn't. All I saw was Vicky, the beautiful smiling young girl listening to Fleetwood Mac, twirling around in a flowing skirt pretending she was Stevie Nicks.

My chest got tight, and tears covered my eyes. I was crying big ugly tears. Vicky got sad and looked down.

"If you can't quit crying... You can't come here again," she said.

"I will. I just want to make sure you are okay." I took a deep breath and cleared my eyes. But the sight of Vicky in her jail uniform, helpless and naïve, broke me.

"I'm fine. I have food and a bathroom. My attorney says they are putting in for a venue change, and I'll be going to Dunklin County, Missouri. That is in Kennett, you know, where Sheryl Crow is from. She might do a concert in the jail, you never know."

Even in jail, she was all about music. I tried to think of something else besides Vicky's vulnerability.

"Vicky, there is something I wanted to ask you about Kenny. Did you know the doctor said he was schizophrenic?"

"No, but I knew there was something wrong with him. He used to say a Missouri State Highway Patrol trooper was stalking him. He would say the trooper was outside his house and looking in his windows. I just thought it was his drinking."

"No, he was taking some pills; he said they were vitamins. I don't know," I replied.

"Time's up. Back to your cell," the officer yelled.

"I gotta go back. I got those papers signed and notarized. I will give them to the officer to give you, so stay around here. I love you, sissy."

She hadn't told me she loved me in years. "I love you too."

She danced and waved as she walked back to her cell. *Rock on, Gold Dust Woman*—your little sister is here to help you.

Me, Poplar Bluff, Missouri 1979

CHAPTER THREE

I was in the second grade when I learned I was white trash. I was attending a small, all-white country school, and it was during coloring time that I listened to two girls that I considered my friends discuss a birthday party the weekend before. I had not been invited. I didn't understand why. Or what I did that made them not ask me.

"My mom doesn't like your mom. Y'all are white trash," explained the birthday girl matter-of-factly.

I didn't know exactly what that meant. I knew the words were something bad, and I was it. I asked the girls to tell me what that meant.

"You all are poor and don't have a father. My mom says your mom is a loudmouth with a bad temper who beats everyone up. You know—white trash."

As a child, I equated kindness with pity. The older ladies at church were nice to me, but I could see how they felt sorry for me with my dirty fingernails and old rummage sale dress. I never had tights or stockings like the other girls, but I would spend hours reading and learning the Bible, hoping that they would not look down on me. I worked hard to learn all the books of the New Testament and even made up a song to impress them.

Mom saw people who were kind and compassionate as weak. The Merle Haggard tune "Fightin' Side of Me" was her personal theme song. She didn't understand why people wouldn't fight back when they were disrespected.

This was directly the opposite of my church learning. I strived to be Christ-like and love my neighbor, and not raise a hand to anyone. When I was on the sidelines of one of Mom's many verbal and physical fights, I would think about Galatians 5:15: *But if you bite and devour one another, watch out that you are not consumed by one another.*

I never knew the true meaning of kindness and compassion until I met Edna Hastings. She became a part of my extended family when my older sister Trixie married her son. They had been dating since high school, but she got pregnant before they were married, and Mom had a meltdown. She telephoned the Hastings' home and cussed Edna and Mr. Hastings out, blaming them for my sister's pregnancy. Edna didn't hang up or get angry, and Mom didn't know how to handle this; she was used to settling things with her fists. Edna just stayed on the phone, listening patiently while Mom threatened and cursed their entire family.

A couple of years later, Mom went back to work nights and asked my older sister Trixie to babysit me. My brother-in-law was going to college, and the young family was living with Edna to save money. Edna was a pretty, heavy-set woman and always had a smile on her face. I loved going to Edna's. Her home was a tiny brick house on Raulston Street in North Poplar Bluff. It was clean, and everything matched. I hadn't known stores even made towels in sets of the same color. Ours were a mix from yard sales and thrift stores. What I really enjoyed at Edna's was the routine. She always checked if I had homework. We had a warm dinner with good home-cooked food every night. When I slept over, she would ask if I brushed my teeth and showered. At home, Mom never asked; she would just yell if it wasn't done.

Edna was the polar opposite of Mom. Edna was kind and not afraid to show love to her children. Mom loved but always with conditions. I watched Mom cuss and try to provoke Edna over the phone. Edna would just listen and never said a mean word about her. I never heard her talk bad about anyone. I would often look at Edna and say to myself that I wanted to be as caring as her.

Rural women are supposed to be quiet and subservient, and to rely on a man. Mom didn't know her place in that kind of society, or if she did, she rejected it. Mom was only calm when plotting revenge or deciding where to hit you so it would cause the most pain. She often would tell me, "Betty, don't let no one tell you what to do—especially a man."

When I was nine years old, I accompanied Mom to the large weekly outdoor flea market and livestock auction called the Sale Barn. Every Friday, vendors would set up tables outside the auction area to sell everything from ducks to clothes. While we were looking at the tables, Mom saw Rosie, a woman she worked with, who wasn't too much bigger than me. Rosie looked like she was crying and arguing with the man walking beside her. The man, who had at least two feet and over a couple hundred pounds on Rosie, started talking in a loud voice. Then he kicked Rosie in her back, causing her to fall toward the end of a pickup truck. He spun her around and put his finger in her face. The whole crowd of about 30 people, men and women, turned around, but only Mom approached them.

"Rosie, you okay?" Mom asked.

"Oh, Mary. I am fine," Rosie said with a fake smile holding her back.

"She is fine," the man replied.

"Johnny, she don't look fine," Mom said.

"She is fine," he answered.

"Rosie, you okay, do you need me to call someone? I can call your mom," Mom said.

"No, Mary, I am okay," Rosie answered in a voice almost as tiny as she was.

"She is my wife, and she is fine," Johnny replied.

"Then why did you push her?" Mom asked.

"Well... she just ain't been acting right. Acts like she is uppity since she works now," the man said.

Mom moved in front of the man toward Rosie.

"Act right? If you acted right and kept a job instead of drinking, you would have a paycheck too," Mom said.

The man moved between Mom and Rosie.

"Mary, you need to mind your own business," the man said.

"Make me," Mom said, getting close to the man's face.

The man turned away from Mom and raised his left hand, then threw it to the ground.

Mom persisted.

"Make me. If you think you can, then try. You son of a bitch. I am no little hundred-pound girl." The man turned around and put his fist up like he was going to hit Mom.

Mom, Poplar Bluff, Missouri 1970

Mom just smiled and got further in his face.

"Hit me and see where you land, motherfucker," Mom said.

The man contemplated it and turned away. Rosie stood there with tears in her eyes.

"It will be okay, Mary. I will go home, and everything will be okay."

"You don't have to go with him. As long as I have a home, you do too," Mom said.

"No, it is okay." Rosie got in the truck.

Johnny turned and looked at Mom like he won some sort of prize.

"Don't look at me, you bastard. I will knock your teeth out of your head," Mom yelled as the truck spun a little gravel pulling out. Mom swung her purse and hit the tailgate of the truck.

Rosie looked over her shoulder one more time at Mom as if to say she was sorry. As the truck drove out of sight, Mom scanned the crowd, trying to find somewhere to place her anger and frustration.

"Betty, look at all these cowards. Let a little woman get the hell beat out of her. But come Sunday, they all can go to church and play like they are Christians," Mom yelled at the top of her voice. No one in the crowd said anything to Mom.

When we got back in Mom's truck, she turned to me and said, "Don't you ever let anyone tell you how to act. God gave you a voice... use it."

I had let the harsh words hurled by my childhood classmates define me for years. I thought I had left those hurts behind me when I left Poplar Bluff, but the wounds beneath those scars were fresher than I thought. I had worked so hard to build a life built on love and compassion. I forged a successful career in law enforcement that reflected my liberal values. I thought I had taken the best parts of my Mom, her strength and tenacious spirit, and integrated them with the patience and kindness learned at Edna Hastings' kitchen table to be a better person. Better than Mom and my sisters and brothers all hell-bent on destruction. Better than those who hurt children while consumed with drugs and rage. I had left this place and these people behind me. Coming back to rural Missouri to deal with Vicky's case tore at the invisible scars and left those old wounds wide open.

As soon as I retrieved the signed Power of Attorney paperwork, I wanted to get Vicky's vehicles back from the Isaac family. The cars were the only assets Vicky owned outright, and I needed to protect their value. Whether or not the probate court would later decide to split ownership with the Isaacs was not my concern; Vicky legally owned the cars. Chris' brothers had already made not entirely truthful statements to the police. I had to be strategic and prepared.

I drove to the trailer to check on Kenny. He understood that I never wanted to step foot in that house again and met me outside.

"Did you see ol' prisoner 'I'? You know that is what they call her because her last name starts with an 'I.'" He laughed. Kenny always smiled, flashing his beautiful, straight teeth. Vicky has the same straight teeth.

"She was fine. Almost dancing to the phone to talk."

"She wasn't showing her ass, was she?"

"No, but she was happier than I've seen her in a long time."

"Ain't that some stuff? Goin' to jail and dancing. Don't she know she might not ever get out? With her crazy ass."

"I know... Do you need anything before I go back?"

"Well, I got a paper I want you to take a look at. I gotta go get it," he said, walking back into the trailer.

I cringed just thinking about him going back into that stinking filth. At least Mom wasn't alive to see Kenny living like this. Kenny suddenly opened the dirty metal door, and his size 13 shoes traipsed out.

"They gonna cut the electric off in two weeks if it ain't paid," Kenny said, exiting the house with the disconnect notice.

"How much is it?" I asked.

"$387.86. It looks like they haven't paid this in a couple of months."

"Well, we'll come up with it somehow."

"She said she had her last Social Security check on her card with her stuff in evidence."

"That would be good because they left a lot of bills."

"Oh, and here is a letter from the Bank of Advance on their missed house payments this month."

"Okay. Just give me all that information. I'll deal with it."

"She left you a mess, didn't she?" he laughed.

"What a damn mess."

Kenny was shaking more than his usual "bird calls." I had another call to make: to the crime victims compensation service in Jefferson City, Missouri, to get him some counseling. Standing there looking at him, I couldn't differentiate between the adult Kenny who might have killed his stepfather and the little boy who didn't learn how to read until he was 11 years old. Counseling might help him deal with anything he may have witnessed, or it might reveal his involvement.

Another reason I went to the trailer was to get Snowball. One of the Isaacs returned her to Kenny after she bit or tried to bite someone. She looked haggard and had a cut on her face. I put her in the car and drove to the vet to get her examined. I hoped nothing else was wrong with the poor dog and that the cut wasn't from abuse. If anyone had hurt her, I would have filed charges in a minute. The dog was an innocent in this whole mess. Luckily, the doctor assured me it was from an untreated skin condition.

As we drove the three hours back toward St. Louis, Snowball reminded me of Vicky, a tough exterior but a loving soul. She was a friendly, sweet dog. Her nose soaked up my car's air conditioner. She looked up at me as if to smile and thank me. I found a veterinarian friend with three acres of land that was a dreamland for dogs to run and play. He agreed to adopt Snowball. She would be free and not tied to a post with a massive log chain in a tiny front yard. If only I could do that for Vicky.

The next morning my first call was to the Crime Victims Compensation Department on behalf of Kenny. The State of Missouri provides financial assistance for people who suffered physical, emotional, or mental harm or trauma resulting from a crime. This includes counseling expenses for family members living with a victim or who are witnesses to the crime. They also assist in funeral and burial expenses if the person is killed during a crime. The counselor told me to fill out the application found on the internet.

"Is this the Chris Isaac case from Puxico?" the counselor asked.

71

"Yes, do you know the case?"

"Yes, his brother and father applied for funeral benefits, and I've been trying to reach them. I called and sent them a letter advising them that all the application is missing is the death certificate. If they want help with the funeral expenses, we can help."

"Really. Well, I don't speak to them. So, you might want to try to call them or send another letter because they have been trying to raise funds for the funeral."

"Yes. But I have tried many times. Thank you. We look forward to helping your nephew."

"Thank you."

I pondered this news. Elmer held a fundraiser for the funeral. Chris' sister Angelica's church also raised funds. People who are more willing to take money collected from the community and friends than $5,000 from a state program funded by the fines and court costs from those found guilty were not seeking justice. In my view, they were seeking admiration at the expense of their deceased loved one.

My next call was the Stoddard County Sheriff's office to get access to Vicky's bank card. I asked to speak with Sheriff Carl Hefner. I didn't know him personally as we hadn't worked together when I was a chief, though I had worked in all the surrounding counties as a deputy.

"This is Deputy Golden. Can I help you?"

"I need to get my sister Vicky Isaac's bank card out of evidence. Her son is disabled and has no other way to support himself. What is the process for doing that?"

"So how are we supposed to help her? Maybe she shouldn't be in jail and taking care of her kid."

"What does that mean?"

"People who commit crimes go to jail and don't get special treatment."

I wasn't asking for anything. I just wanted to know what the procedure was to get her property. Vicky was awaiting trial and had not yet been convicted of anything. As police officers, we just enforce the law. We are not judges.

72

"Excuse me. Everyone gets his or her day in court." I could feel my blood boil.

"What is your name, ma'am?"

"Betty Frizzell."

"Hold on."

The line went silent. I thought this was abrupt but took a breath and remembered being on the other side. It could be that the deputy was having a bad day dealing with surly people in lock-up, or maybe that was just his demeanor. Oftentimes, people working in the criminal justice system tend to lose our manners because we are bigger-picture people—coming off as rude but always thinking of the future and how things will end up. We see so many criminals. It becomes hard to see citizens.

"You will need to talk to the prosecutor." The phone went dead. He hung up on me.

I was working to keep my temper under control and called the prosecutor's office. The prosecutor would have to give permission to the Sheriff's office. I assumed that I would be given the same respect I get in other sheriff offices across the state who recognized me as a fellow officer. When I worked with fellow law enforcement, jails, and prosecutors, I treated everyone with mutual respect. I viewed other departments as an extension of my own department—all for the greater good. The next phone call told me that Stoddard County did not consider me a part of the fraternity.

"Hello, my name is Betty Frizzell, and I would like to speak to someone about evidence."

"Yes. What do you need to know?" said the male voice on the other end.

"My sister is in the Stoddard County Jail, and I need to get her bank card out of evidence to help her son pay her bills. He is disabled and has no means to support himself."

"What is her name?"

"Vicky Isaac."

"Yeah, we aren't going to discuss this with you. Her attorney will have to make a request." Again, the phone went dead.

"What?"

I checked my phone. He'd hung up on me too.

I experienced what millions of citizens in rural counties face daily. A casual bias and discriminatory attitude based on assumptions about a person's family and poverty is why many crime victims don't come forward in rural counties. Besides the lack of privacy and the financial barriers rural citizens experience, the fear of being treated like a criminal or not being believed allows them to be victimized and revictimized. Victims feel they are not worthy enough to receive the same protection as other citizens with wealth and influence.

Vicky's attorney advised me to send him a letter stating precisely what she wanted released, and he would take it up with the prosecutor. This process could take up to three weeks to get a response from the prosecutor's office. From my experience, this was an unnecessary step; her bank card wasn't pertinent to the case.

I sat in my frustration. My phone rang.

"Heh, Aunt Betty. You busy?" said Kenny.

"No. Just making calls. What's the matter?" I said, praying for not another calamity I would have to handle from hundreds of miles away.

"I ran into Elmer Isaac in town. He said Sheriff Hefner gave him and Chris' dad Chris' card and they got his last Social Security check."

"What? When did this happen?"

"On May 22."

"Okay. I'll call you back."

I called the Social Security Administration to find out more about the legality of this and file a fraud complaint if necessary. As I was on hold waiting to speak to a live person, my rage was burning. I advised the Social Security Administration of the date of Chris' death, May 12th. According to the Social Security personnel, on May 22, 2013, someone withdrew $1,000.00 from an ATM in Bloomfield, Missouri. Donald and Elmer Isaac were the only people with access to the card. I filed a fraud complaint.

I called Kenny back.

"Hello," he said.

"He was telling the truth. Somebody emptied Chris' Social Security account."

"Well, I'll be damned... Does that mean I can get her card to help with these bills?"

"I don't think so. The prosecutor's office is not very cooperative."

"Yeah. That is Stoddard County."

Vicky and Chris' bills were piling up, and we were left to pay them. Kenny had no means of support until he was finally approved for Social Security. I couldn't begin to understand the reasoning behind the Sheriff and prosecutor's offices' refusal to let Vicky have access to her ATM card but allowing the Isaacs to have Chris'.

I hadn't felt like defeated white trash for many years. The treatment I received reminded me of being a little dirty buck-toothed country girl who cried when she wasn't invited to birthday parties. I tried to sleep, but by 4 a.m. I was still awake. I kept thinking of Kenny. Not adult Kenny, but of him being a helpless little boy doing his "bird calls" in the front yard. One of Mom's pigeons out of its flock, alone in hostile territory. I couldn't quit thinking about Kenny alone in that town living in that disgusting house.

Mom left Kenny financially sound when she died. He was her only beneficiary and was left a house, ten acres, and a paid-off car. He didn't have any expenses but the utilities. He was 21 years old and had just begun working for Tyson's Chicken factory. This was also the first time I noticed a change in Kenny. About four months after her funeral, I went back to Poplar Bluff to visit him. When I pulled up to the house, we noticed Kenny had dyed his naturally blond-brown hair dark black. He was calling himself Henry Rodriguez and using a tongue roll to pronounce letters every few syllables. In his refrigerator, there were Mexican TV dinners and tacos. We just thought he was kidding around, trying to be funny. He always had an odd sense of humor.

Personal relationships were never easy for Kenny, especially with the opposite sex. He seemed to attract older and emotionally vulnerable women. He met his first girlfriend at work after Mom died. She was married and 12 years older than him. She was drawn to his likable façade, and Kenny, like other narcissists, liked her emotional expressiveness and nurturing personality. The relationship was mainly sexual. It didn't take long before the sex and alcohol wore off, and the relationship ended. When they broke up, the lady abruptly quit her job at Tyson's. We found out later that she gave birth to a child that was most likely Kenny's. But she was still legally married to her husband, which meant Kenny had no parental rights and never pursued meeting the child. In 2008, Kenny married a woman nearly 20 years older, but that lasted only a few months. He was working on a riverboat and drinking heavily. She cheated on him while he was away working. It wasn't a healthy relationship. After their divorce, Kenny saw a few people, but nothing ever lasted. Kenny didn't talk about dating, marriage, or having children.

I prayed for Mom's strength and cursed her bullying ways. None of this would be going on if she were here to yell, command, and bully everyone into doing the right-enough thing. But then none of this would be going on if she had treated Vicky with love and kindness. What good was there to be had by wishing and hoping the past had been different? Still, I made a promise to Mom to take care of Vicky and Kenny. I was trying my damnedest.

In the next few days, I received calls and letters from Vicky. She now seemed to understand what was going on around her. I dreaded telling her about the electric bill.

"Heh, Kenny got a disconnect notice from the electric company. They said the account hasn't been paid on in a few months."

"What? I gave Chris the money to pay on it last month," Vicky said.

"Well, he didn't. Now we have less than two weeks to get it paid. Maybe you could ask if you could get your card to pay it? I tried, and they said I have to write a letter to the prosecutor, and it could take up to three weeks."

"I'll ask, and I'll send you a letter telling them to release it for Kenny."

"Enough about what is going on out here. How are you doing in there?"

"I'm really hungry. They feed us, but I get hungry during the day. Can you put some money on my books?" Vicky said.

"I will try. How much do you need?"

"Not much. $20 or so."

"Okay. How do I do it?"

"You have to use the company on the internet or send a money order."

"Give me the website, and I'll see if I have any money left."

I was interested in finding out more about this commissary website. It turned out to be another slap in the face. Again, I was forced to be a part of a system that supports a monopolizing company. Families don't get to ask questions about how these prices are set. If a loved one is in jail, you have to pay for them to get hygiene products, snacks, and even toilet paper. The company's prices are exorbitant compared to the outside world; for example, a shampoo bottle that costs $0.88 at a local drugstore is $2.00 or $3.00 at the commissary. On top of that, the local jail gets a percentage of the total amount spent through the inmate commissary accounts. It's sold as a tax savings to citizens but has become a revenue source for many police departments.

Vicky's case was costing me a lot of money. I had to make sure Kenny had food and money to live on, and Vicky and Chris' bills were suffocating me. They were behind on everything—the house payment, the utilities. Where did their money go? Their house payment was only $375 a month. I called the Bank of Advance to talk to their loan officer. He let me know that they had insurance, and if I could get Chris' death certificate, he could file the paperwork to have the mortgage paid off. That was a godsend. But the two Ford Ranger pickups and Vicky's Park Avenue Electra were at Chris' brother's house. Until they were in my possession,

I wasn't paying a dime on those truck notes. I didn't really care much about those trucks, but Vicky's name was on the loan. But I wanted Vicky's Park Avenue Electra back because she outright owned it.

Vicky cared for many things in her life but loved very few. Mom's love was like the Walmart return policy—it could be taken back at any time. We coped by never getting too attached to anything because you never knew when it would be taken away or would leave. Besides her dogs, that 2003 emerald-green Park Avenue Electra was her most prized possession. Even though it was over ten years old when she bought it, it was the newest car she ever owned. Buying it with her own money filled her with pride. She called me the minute she drove it off the lot.

"Heh, sis, I got my Park Avenue Electra, and it is mine. Not the bank's. Not some finance company's. It is mine."

Since she purchased it with her own money, she could limit Chris' access to it. He was known for being rough on vehicles. She convinced him that the Park Avenue Electra was only to be used for special occasions like driving her to the doctor or a family function.

I asked my three older siblings to help with Vicky's expenses, but they refused to talk to me about it. My sister Sylvie in Louisiana screamed at me, "Vicky can rot in jail for all I care." My sister Trixie in Georgia told me not to call her anymore, or she was calling the Sheriff's Department. Trixie was embarrassed because she knew how bad the situation with Vicky and Chris was in early 2013. I warned her in the weeks before the murder that something would happen unless the family intervened. She told me to mind my own business. My brother Butch hates cops so much he doesn't like that I chose a career in law enforcement. One family Thanksgiving after I returned to Missouri, he refused to eat dinner with me, telling Mom, "I don't eat dinner with no pigs." I was on my own as usual.

When I sent Vicky money, I sure wouldn't mail a money order to the jail. It was common knowledge in Missouri law enforcement circles that Stoddard County had bookkeeping problems. During a 2010 audit of Stoddard County, the State of Missouri Auditor found that the Sheriff's Department did not maintain records of inmates' commissary purchases or balances. The report also stated the Sheriff's Department did not keep adequate records or follow procedures regarding the commissary inventory.

That wasn't the only incident. While Vicky was in the Stoddard County Jail, the former office manager was arrested for stealing from the commissary accounts. This was a person who had lived in Puxico and worked for the Sheriff's Department for 22 years yet still stole $14,867. In a news conference, Missouri State Auditor Tom Schweich found the discrepancies during a 2013 audit. Still, Sheriff Hefner claimed he got a confession from the employee about the theft *before* the auditor found the missing funds. Schweich was gracious and gave Sheriff Hefner credit for working with his office during the investigation. Still, Sheriff Hefner continued to claim he was right and found the stolen money first... after 22 years of the office manager embezzling it under his nose.

In Missouri, a Sheriff has the distinction of being the county's chief law enforcement; only the coroner can arrest a Sheriff. The Sheriff's attitude sets the tone for the rest of the department, and continuing an argument with the state auditor for the sake of being right was no way to promote community trust. I got more worried. If this was how he treated a colleague, Vicky didn't stand much of a chance with the county court.

I waited for Vicky's call on Sunday to see if there was any movement helping Kenny with the electric bill. We were running out of time before they disconnected power. She called later that night, and I hoped she had some good news.

"Hey, sis. What are you doing?"

"Nothing. How are you? Did you get that money I put on your commissary?"

"I'm fine. Yes, I got it. And I put my check on my books, so you don't have to send me any money. Kenny can come up to the jail and get some money for the electric bill."

"What? What do you mean you put your check on your books?"

"I put my whole check on my books?"

"How? Do they have an ATM in the jail?"

I was confused. There is no way in hell there is an ATM that the inmates could have access to. It would be emptied out in a heartbeat.

"No, the deputies took me to the ATM down the road and let me withdraw my money for Kenny," Vicky said like a proud schoolgirl who just brought home a report card with straight A's.

"What the hell are you talking about? You were taken to the ATM? You have no bond because you are a danger to yourself and others. But you went to the ATM? How the fuck did you get taken out of the jail?" The nerve in my forehead that starts my migraines bulged and throbbed.

"I told the Sheriff I had money on my card and needed to give it to my son. They handcuffed me, and a deputy took me to the ATM. I took the money out and put the entire $1,000 on my books. What is the matter?"

"Vicky, once you put that money on your books, you can only spend it at the jail. They wanted you to do that because they make money off of what you spend. There is no way Kenny can get any money from that."

"Oh, I thought I was doing the right thing." She sounded defeated.

"It is okay. I have to go talk to Kenny." I just wanted off a recorded phone line before the deputies heard my cussword-laced opinion about what they had just done.

"I tried, Betty..." she said in her scolded little girl voice.

"I know you did. You were just given the wrong information. The sooner we get you a change of venue, the better," I said, as my lower jaw tightened holding back my anger.

"I love you, sissy."

"I love you too."

A full-blown migraine percolated. I didn't have time for headaches. I was stunned. The Sheriff's Department took Vicky, a person on a no-bond first-degree murder warrant, that a judge declared a danger to herself and others, to a public ATM and had her withdraw her entire Social Security check and put it on her books. I knew exactly why—because every purchase she makes with that money on her commissary account profits the department.

I wanted to call the Sheriff's office and cuss everyone out. They didn't care about me being a fellow officer. I was just a murderer's sister down there. They made me aware of that time and time again. I took a deep breath to clear out the anger.

A day of rest gave me more clarity. I wanted to speak with the Sheriff, and I knew that Missouri is a one-party consent state, which means only one party has to consent to being recorded during a phone call. I consented.

Three days later, after numerous calls, I finally got Sheriff Hefner on the phone. At first, the conversation was cordial; he said Vicky was in no danger because two officers took her to the ATM. I told him of my background and explained my concern for his officers' safety because the Isaac family threatened to kill Vicky if she was let out of jail. "I have been an officer my entire adult life. I don't think I would have let my officers be in such a situation given the threats by the victim's family."

I think this struck a nerve. How dare someone from St. Louis tell him how to conduct his business? His last words to me: "Maybe you should stay up in St. Louis and not worry about what is going on in Stoddard County." Then he hung up on me.

I played the tape back and listened to the recorded conversation. I was an outsider and would always be an outsider. This was not the glass ceiling I fought to break for so many years of my career. This was a steel wall. I couldn't solve a crime spree or arrest a serial child molester to get respect because respect was not earned in this community. Mind my business and stay out of Stoddard County was his message and final word.

If I was going to have any impact, I needed to go public. I spoke with veteran reporter Kathy Sweeney of Channel 12 KFVS, the station everyone in southeastern Missouri watched for news. After telling her about Vicky being taken to the ATM, she wanted to hear the tape and confirm I was really a former police chief and criminal justice professor. I sent her my contact information along with a copy of the taped conversation.

The next day Sweeney called to ask if I could come down to the news station in Cape Girardeau, Missouri, for an interview. Julian and I drove the hundred-mile trip the following day at 2 p.m. I told Kenny about the film date, and he wanted to come with us—all of this costing more time and more money than I had.

When I picked up Kenny, I realized how his personality disorders had taken over control of his life. He wore slacks and a button-up long-sleeve shirt. I asked Kenny why he was so dressed up. He said, in case "Ol' Sweeney had any questions" for him. During the 70-mile drive from Puxico, Missouri, to the news station in Cape Girardeau, Kenny kept listening to the tape over and over again.

The news station building outside looked as old as the Mississippi River flowing nearby. The building's inside was painted with sterile colors with the letters "KFVS 12" in shiny silver letters. The reporter interviewed me as a cameraman filmed, and I showed the letter from Vicky and the pictures of us together. I wanted to make sure that this was not a smear piece against all police but focused directly on Sheriff Hefner, and made the public aware that his department did not follow proper protocol for my sister and his officers' safety.

Sheriff Hefner was given his opportunity to tell his version of the story. He looked like every other Sheriff I had known, dressed in his country brown with a shiny badge, as he attempted to turn the outrageous act of removing Vicky from the jail for their revenue gain back on our family. Sheriff Hefner made the statement, "I don't know why they needed the money so bad." On the recorded conversation tape, I told him about Kenny having no means of support. Also, he ended his piece saying, "If she didn't have any money on her books, the taxpayer would have to pay for her." This is not true; if an inmate doesn't have money, they cannot buy anything.

The interview aired a few days later. I received an email from Sweeney telling me that Sheriff Hefner claimed he had a video of the two officers taking Vicky to the ATM, but Sweeney said she viewed the video, and it only showed one officer. Sweeney reached out to the Stoddard County Prosecutor Ross Oliver, but he declined to comment on the situation. I felt the news piece was fair and portrayed the information in the correct light.

After the piece aired, I received an email from Kathy Sweeney that the Isaac family called her and the station with profanity-laced abuse and criticism. They wanted to tell their side of the story, but their grieving had nothing to do with Vicky being taken to an ATM so the Sheriff's Department could access her money. They vowed revenge on me. I thought of the quote from Aesop, "He who plots to hurt others often hurts himself."

The news program did get one thing accomplished—Vicky got her change of venue and was moved out of Stoddard County into the custody of the Dunklin County Sheriff's Department.

CHAPTER FOUR

 Vicky quickly adjusted to the improved conditions in Dunklin County Jail. She didn't fear retaliation and the staff was competent. The dread I had heard in her voice while she was in the Stoddard County Jail was gone. Vicky told me that the news piece got her more than the jail transfer. She was also assigned a new public defender, Rebecca (Becky) Burke, her third since her arrest. Ms. Burke wasn't happy about my contact with the media.

On Monday morning, I called Ms. Burke to introduce myself and ask where to send the files I picked up from the trailer.

"I wanted to talk to you about this bullshit of you going to the news." She was blunt.

"What bullshit? What does Vicky getting taken to the ATM have to do with her criminal case?"

She was silent.

"Ms. Frizzell, you don't piss off the judges down here. Going to the media and showing up their law enforcement is bad for Vicky."

"I teach my students every day that the criminal justice system's job is to deliver justice. I am fighting for my sister. Are you?"

"Don't tell me how to do my job," she snapped at me.

"I am not telling you how to do your job but don't tell me how to be a sister. You have no idea what she and I've been through as children."

After an awkward pause, she continued, "Ms. Frizzell, I just want Vicky to get a fair trial."

"You think Vicky isn't? There is no way in hell she is gonna get a fair shake, but I want enough evidence to get an appeal."

She knew what I was saying was the truth. Chris' extended family had vowed revenge and was going to make sure Vicky suffered for what they believed she did.

"I have five banker boxes of medical evidence," she said.

"The more there is, the more to dispute. I am going to send

Vicky and Me, Poplar Bluff, Missouri 1982

you what I have. I sent an email to the Battered Women's Defense Fund in Philadelphia to see if they can assist you."

"I am sorry we got off on the wrong foot. I will do my best for Vicky."

"I accept your apology, but you have to understand I am going to be watching over this case. I am not going anywhere."

"That's fine; please send me what you have. I was going to call you this week to get some information about Vicky's past. I need to know about everything."

Ms. Burke immediately recognized that Vicky's extensive brain damage made it difficult for her to answer questions. Ms. Burke wanted to know if Vicky had domestic violence in her past. I couldn't think of *any* of her relationships where she didn't experience abuse.

A child of abuse is a keeper of secrets. Mom would tell us not to talk about what went on at our house. Obedience was enforced with physical violence and the threat of being sent to the local orphanage, Edgewood Children's Home. When Vicky went to school with bruises, she was instructed to tell anyone who asked that she caused them with her clumsiness or that she fell on her bicycle, or it happened when she took care of the animals. As Mom said, "You don't tell these people what happens here. It stays here."

In personal relationships, the instinctual reflex to keep everything inside was eroding my mental health. I never learned to effectively communicate my feelings or even give voice to boundaries. To help Vicky, I would have to break Mom's cardinal rule and tell everyone what happened in our house and in Vicky and Chris' dysfunctional relationship.

One of my first childhood memories is of Mom beating Vicky. As I played outside of our trailer, I couldn't see Mom, but I heard her yelling:

"Why do you always have to show your ass? Constantly getting on my nerves."

Whack whack... more cracking. It sounded like a tree branch hitting against skin.

"What in the hell is wrong with you? You never listen."

Again, whack whack... crack crack...

Quietly creeping around the side of the trailer, I saw Mom with her right arm extended in the air; her tattooed, worn hands held a tattered, broken quarter-width size tree branch. The branch made a whacking sound when it hit the back of Vicky's exposed thighs. Vicky stood there, not moving, her jaw clenched. Every muscle in her body stood firm. Even while Mom tried to provoke her with harsh words, she stood stone-faced in the Missouri heat and humidity that fueled Mom's anger while it also exhausted her, sapping her rage until she released the branch. "Nothing can get through your thick head."

A bright red line ran from the bottom of Vicky's shorts down each of her thighs, disappearing into her socks. First on the right leg, and then the left leg.

"See what you made me do? Cut blood out of you," Mom said as she shoved Vicky.

Mom wiped the sweat from her forehead and walked toward the trailer, gasping as she went. I froze, waiting to hear the door shut behind her.

I ran to Vicky.

"You okay?" I asked.

Vicky looked ahead and did not acknowledge my voice.

"You hurt?"

Vicky's face looked forward into the woods. Her upper lip sat swollen on her lower lip. She lumbered and limped to the clothesline and reached for a washcloth. A faint "ouch" escaped her mouth.

"What you doin'? Your legs are bleeding."

Vicky remained silent as she cleaned the blood off her legs and threw the washcloth into the trash burn barrel, tossed aside like she was after the beating. Vicky never mumbled a word, then walked into the woods, not to be seen again for hours.

As Vicky matured into a young woman, any thoughts of romantic love were dictated by Mom. Her advice about sex was, "If you do it, I will kill you." With all Mom's failed relationships, her directive seemed like hypocrisy. It was acceptable for us to wear makeup and flirt, but there was no such thing as harmless curiosity. Mom called us girls "a regular little whore" for being too flirtatious. Our virginity was sacred, and if we lost it before getting married, we were considered damaged goods. These were the same views held by Roxie, her religious mother.

The church we attended perpetuated Mom's basic principles. It taught that marriage was a lifelong commitment strictly between a man and a woman. God gifted the marital union so that the married man and woman could have an intimate relationship for procreation. Women were supposed to obey God, their fathers, and then their husbands. Women weren't even allowed to preach in our churches. There wasn't much room for "women's liberation." The religious norms and expectations made disclosure of sexual abuse difficult. Sexual assault victims were expected to suffer silently, with the abuse seen as a cross that they simply had to bear. Children raised in these religious traditions are encouraged to pray for the abuse to stop and accept their abuse as "fate" if it continues.

Incest was accepted as a consequence of being born a female. Our oldest sister, Jackie, told our Grandma Roxie she was raped by one of our uncles. Grandma Roxie beat her with a leather belt for talking about such wickedness. Vicky had been sexually assaulted by our brother. She and her small puppy were playing on the couch. Our older brother Butch sat next to her on the sofa, watching television. He asked Vicky to sit on his lap. Vicky, with the puppy in her hand, sat on his lap. He covered Vicky and the puppy with a blanket and started moving Vicky up and down on his lap. Vicky tried to get free when the puppy started whimpering, but our brother was too strong. He held her and the puppy until he ejaculated. When he finally released Vicky, she checked on her puppy, but the dog had been smothered to death under the blanket. Our brother told Mom that Vicky accidentally killed the puppy. For years, Vicky believed it was her fault the puppy died.

Butch continued to sexually abuse Vicky for the next decade until she was about 14. I did not know this until years later, when I learned that was the reason Mom sent Vicky to live with our older sister Sylvie for a year.

Vicky was also raped as a teenager at a friend's house party. An older brother of the friend drugged Vicky's drink. She passed out, and the three brothers sexually assaulted her. Mom had found her, partially clothed, and passed out on the stairs of the apartment. Mom took her to the local hospital, where the trauma team had a rape kit done to collect evidence as they pumped her stomach. Vicky felt guilt and confusion and embarrassment. She didn't want doctors or nurses touching her, and she didn't want to talk about the repeated abuse she suffered. Although Mom reported the rape to the police, the brothers were not arrested because Vicky ultimately refused to cooperate with authorities.

Her cognitive limitations and the warped view of sexuality shaped by Mom made her feel that everything that happened to her was her fault. That she caused the bicycle accident that scarred her pelvic region, because she had to be punished for allowing herself to be abused as a child. That her puppy's death was her fault too. That being gang-raped was her fault for being a "regular little whore." And that to even hope for love in this world was to curse against God.

The new lawyer's call saddened and exhausted me because before Vicky's arrest, I never really thought that much about the abuse Vicky endured. It was just her messy life. Vicky, the one who Mom always beat. Vicky, the one who got black eyes from all her boyfriends. Vicky, the one who lived recklessly and impulsively. This was just who she was. I felt terrible because I never saw her as a domestic violence survivor; I just saw her as my sister, who made bad choices.

My sadness turned into anger at Mom. I never confronted Mom about the abuse because I didn't understand the damage done to me, and of course to Vicky, until I got older. Maybe, too, that's why I loved being in law enforcement; I could experience the chaos

I had become accustomed to seeing every day. Violence was *my* normal too. Except I escaped Mom and Missouri and lulled myself into thinking that I was not damaged by my childhood. I was caught in a complex web of knowing the peaceful life I wanted but not feeling comfortable in that life. Trauma became normalized. I still craved the chaos.

CHAPTER FIVE

I felt that I couldn't do a lot for Vicky, but at least I could get her cars back. It became symbolic. A victory. A return of something she loved to show her that not everything was hopeless.

My husband, son, and I rented a car and drove to Elmer Isaac's house on the outskirts of Puxico. Outside of Elmer's house, I found two of the three cars—the 2001 Ford Ranger and Park Avenue. Both had four flat tires. Vicky's car was half sunken in the muddy field. I wasn't sure we could drive it away and contemplated the extra costs of calling a tow truck.

I called a wrecker service, and they wanted $300 just to drive from Poplar Bluff to Puxico. That was more money than I had. A can of Fix-a-Flat and a tire jack would have to do. Mom had taught me to change a tire in five minutes or quicker.

The plan to get the cars was simple. My husband and I would make two trips to ferry Vicky's cars to the house. For everyone's protection, we brought a video camera that Julian volunteered to operate to document exactly what we were doing. As soon as we turned onto the gravel road in front of Elmer's house, we turned the video camera on and started filming. We parked the rental car on the public gravel road where we saw Elmer working in his garden, using a hoe to clear weeds in the watermelon patch.

Elmer was older than Chris and showed us the pleasant attitude that had impressed Mom so much. He and his wife were frequent churchgoers who lived in a double-wide trailer and didn't chase material things for happiness, but still, he was an Isaac, and I was cautious. He had already talked the Sheriff into giving them Chris' bank card and letting them take things out of the trailer. He often chastised others for not living rightly, while defending or ignoring his own family's illegal goings-on. I needed to be incredibly careful.

"Hello, Elmer, I'm Betty, Vicky's younger sister. Can I speak with you for a minute?" I said from the road, wanting to remain safe from any accusation of trespassing.

He put down the hoe and looked at me.

"Yeah, what can I do you for?" The words rolled slowly out of his mouth. My impression of him has always been that of a hard-working, God-fearing man. Not necessarily book-smart or worldly educated but a decent human being.

"I know Mr. Feeney told you that I filed for power of attorney for Vicky. Since Vicky is still the legal owner of those cars, I need to get them and take them back up to the house." I remained calm and courteous.

He looked as if he was registering what I just told him. "Well, let me see the paperwork," he said, wiping his callused hands on his blue-jean overalls.

"Sure. Feel free to look them over." I kept my voice calm and low-key.

He examined the paperwork to the last word.

"Listen, Elmer, I don't have anything against you. We're both stuck in the middle of a mess. A court will decide the punishment, but in the meantime, the legal owner of those vehicles is wanting them back at the house." That was the truth, but his family had no right to take the cars in the first place. I had negotiated with lots of people, but this was personal.

"Mr. Feeney told me you got these papers done, so I'd know they be proper."

"So, you need to go get the keys, and we will be out of your hair, and you can go back to tending your garden."

"I don't want no trouble," he said.

I felt relieved. "We don't either. We were asked to come get them, and that's that."

"You know she killed Chris, and we are out a lot of money for the funeral. I wanted to keep the cars to help pay for the funeral."

"Well, I can't really talk about that. There will be a court date. But you could have gotten $5,000 from the Crime Victims Compensation Fund if you or your dad send the death certificate in."

"Are you sure they'll give us money?"

"I think they will pay it to the funeral home—not to an individual, but you could call them and see how they do it."

94

"We want the money," he said.

"It doesn't hurt to ask them." I knew from helping families of crime victims that they would not give him a check, but I was trying to keep the peace.

"I'll go get the keys."

"Elmer, why are the tires flat?"

"I let the air out of them so they wouldn't get stolen."

"We brought Fix-a-Flat."

Jimmy started airing up the tires.

Then a young woman emerged from the trailer. "Listen, bitch, you ain't taking those cars anywhere."

"I don't know who you are, but I have the paperwork," I said to her. The woman started filming us on her phone.

"I am going to film you."

"That's fine. It's for your protection and ours." I stayed calm. One thing I learned from being a police officer was how to handle hyper-stress.

"This is Stephanie, my stepdaughter. Now, Betty ain't starting no trouble, so don't start any with her," Elmer said.

"You were the one on TV starting trouble with the sheriff."

"Yes, but I don't start trouble. I just end up finishing it." I could feel my calmness slipping away as she continued yelling.

"You are going to be in big trouble making the law mad."

"That's okay. I make lots of people mad in this life."

As this was going on, Jimmy inflated the tires on all the cars, then quickly drove the truck onto the gravel road and parked it. I drove the Park Avenue from the spot it was sunk in the mud, then Jimmy followed in the rental truck with Julian.

As soon as I opened the door to the Park Avenue, it was apparent that someone had trashed Vicky's car. It smelled of cigarettes and had burn holes on the front seat. The cover of the fuse box hung on the floor, exposing the wiring. Big muddy footprints covered the interior floor carpeting. A huge fist-shaped crack spiderwebbed up the front window like someone had punched the windshield. The engine was running rough, and the suspension felt as if it had been taken out joyriding through fields and had been stripped of parts.

As we rounded the corner on the gravel road, a large SUV barreled toward us. At first, I thought it was a reckless driver, but as we got closer, the SUV slammed on its brakes and slid to a stop in the middle of the road, blocking us. A large, short woman got out with her fists clenched. I recognized her as Chris' sister, Doris. I told my son Julian to keep the camera rolling. I jumped out of the car to do my best to de-escalate this situation.

"You're not taking that vehicle anywhere." Her face was red with rage.

"Yeah, I am. My sister's name is on the title, and I am her power of attorney. So, move your car."

"The bitch sister of yours is nothing, and I should kick your ass," she said, standing on her toes to point her finger in my face.

I looked down at her and said, "I know you all are hurting, but I ain't a part of that. He was your family, and she is my family. If it was reversed, you would be getting his stuff like I am for her."

I tried to be rational with her and find common ground. She wasn't as good-natured as Elmer. She was a methamphetamine and pill addict.

"You're a bitch, and your sister is a murdering whore." She made a fist and pulled back as if she was going to hit me. Her husband, Cletus, jumped out of her vehicle and ran up to me.

Jimmy pulled up behind me, slammed the car into park, and jumped out as he told Julian to stay in the car.

"Don't think about it, motherfucker," Jimmy said to Cletus. "Back up off my wife. You want sooome? We can go throw down right now, cuz."

When I am upset, my country accent comes out. When Jimmy gets angry, he turns 100% streetwise North St. Louis. The sudden appearance of 6'3", two-hundred-pound Jimmy stunned Cletus, causing his hands to shake back and forth as if to say no. Jimmy stayed face to face with him.

"Jimmy, don't worry about these people. She's going to move that car, and we all are going to be on our way," I said.

96

Inside my head, I was furious. I would've liked to punch her in the face. However, I've been cussed at too many times by worse folks than her. I was not going to lose my temper.

"Fuck you, bitch. Your ass is going to get kicked," Doris screamed in my face.

"Well, I guess you have a decision to make." I pointed to her car. "Move that thing or get in a fight. Either way, it is going to be on videotape."

She looked back at my son holding the camera.

"Well, smile pretty for the camera," I said.

"Get back in the truck," Cletus said to her.

"No, I am going to beat this stuck-up bitch's ass and her wigger husband."

"No, come on. Let's just go home. I ain't got no bail money. Come on." Cletus put his arms around her and turned her toward him. "Come on. Let's get." He pulled her back to the truck and guided her to the passenger seat. He moved the truck out of the way as I walked backwards toward the Park Avenue, keeping my eyes on his truck. Jimmy walked to the side of the road.

They drove past me. Doris put her middle finger out and yelled out the window, "Fuck you. Tell Vicky I hope she rots in jail."

"My sister ain't been convicted of anything. You need to remember that."

Jimmy touched my arm. "You okay?"

"Yes, are you?"'

"Man, that dude was a punk-ass bitch. It isn't like I haven't been called a wigger before."

Jimmy and I were used to the labels people put on us—I was white trailer trash, Jimmy was white ghetto trash.

The whole situation was ridiculous. I was dressed in my teaching clothes—conservative professor slacks and a button-up shirt—standing in the middle of a gravel road, ready to fight over a half-wrecked 13-year-old car owned by my accused murderer sister.

When we arrived back at the trailer, I called the Stoddard County Sheriff's Department. The dispatcher said it would be

Kenny and Jim outside the trailer

at least 30 minutes before they contacted us. I noticed Kenny's hands were shaking. I asked him if he was okay, and he nodded his head yes. I wished this day was over, but we still needed to get the Ranger, so Jimmy and I drove back to Elmer's trailer to get the truck.

Now everyone was at Elmer's trailer waiting for us. Elmer, his wife, his stepdaughter Stephanie, his sister Doris and her husband Cletus were standing in the front yard. We stopped the rental car in the middle of the road.

"Well, look at that. What are we gonna do?"

"Get that truck. Fuck them. Let them start something. I have it on tape," said Jimmy as he went to open the door.

Jimmy exited the rental car and pulled the video camera out the window.

"Look at that bitch. She is scared she is going to get her ass kicked. Come on, Stephanie. Let's kick her ass."

Elmer stopped them.

"There ain't gonna be no fighting today," Elmer said, and stood in front of them. "Not with my grandkids in the house." But Elmer was also the person who had called Doris and Cletus to intercept us further down the road with the intent to stop us. I was so tired of these fools.

Jimmy jumped into the Ranger's driver's seat and put in a CD that was to be the signal that he was ready to go. As soon as I heard Eminem sing "I'm Not Afraid," I turned the rental car's ignition and mounted the video camera on the dashboard. We drove the rental car and the truck back to the trailer without any more interference from the Isaacs.

Jimmy and I inspected the cars. The truck was in good working condition. The trunk of the Park Avenue was filled with a ton of Chris' personal papers. Some were medical records, but there was also a notebook with notes in Chris' handwriting. Vicky had told me that Chris had, for a short time, begun seeing a therapist to fulfill a requirement of his Social Security application. The writing was childlike, barely legible, and riddled with spelling errors. In the notes, he outlined the sexual abuse he suffered at the hands of his older siblings. He wrote of how his older sister, Crystal, raped him when he was 12 years old. And that his older siblings Elmer and Angelica starved and beat him when Chris' mother ran off with another man. We were horrified.

The only two things the Isaacs took from the house the day of the murder were the cars and these records and notebooks. I don't know what they were thinking. Perhaps Elmer and Angelica were worried that Chris' stories of abuse might get back to their employers and their church community. In small towns, there are no secrets, but without proof, there is always deniability.

The journal entries made me physically ill. We closed the book and put all the papers away for safekeeping until I could turn them over to Vicky's lawyer. I was exhausted. It wasn't the adrenaline of the confrontation as much as it was the realization that Vicky and Chris experienced the same type of abuse as children. Like so many people who never get therapeutic help to find healthy ways to deal with trauma, they continued the cycle of abuse and self-destruction. Chris became the abuser to Vicky's perpetual victim.

All of this—the fighting, the jails, the poverty, the drug abuse, the incest, the criminality—was pulling me back into a world I worked so hard to escape. Yes, I grew up here. And yes, I came from these people, but I was not *like* them. I didn't want to be like them.

The next day, I took Kenny to visit Vicky in Kennett, Missouri. Right before you cross into the town limits, the fields blow pieces of fluffy white cotton, piled ankle-high along the side of the road. The city sign reads, "Welcome to Kennett, Missouri, Home of Sheryl Crow." It's a small farming town of about 10,000 people south of Poplar Bluff, but it didn't evoke the same depressing feelings as Puxico did in me.

The jail, located on a side street in town, was more modern than the Stoddard County Jail. The metal building looked like it could be an outlet store or a warehouse. White lettering outlined in blue read "Dunklin County Justice Center." A looming radio tower stood on the building's side like a homing beacon for the area police. There was a huge mobile command center parked to the side of the building.

The visiting room was full of people. We spoke to Vicky on the phone with glass separating us. She looked happy to see us. She said this jail was much better, and she was no longer worried about Chris' family doing anything to her, which was her haunting fear back in Stoddard County. We told her about how we retrieved her cars without going into details about the run-in with Doris and Cletus.

It was a brief visit. As we were leaving, she told Kenny she loved him. I didn't hear Kenny tell her he loved her back. I can't remember ever hearing him say that he loved her. I was only now realizing this. I was more convinced than ever that Vicky made the ultimate sacrifice for her son and taken responsibility for a murder she didn't commit.

The health department finally sent me the notarized copies of Chris' death certificate—the official cause was ten shots to the head. Kenny told us he only heard six of the ten. The gun held six rounds. If the events happened as detailed in the police report, it meant Vicky emptied all six bullets in the chamber into her sleeping husband, then walked across the room to get the box of shells that sat on the top of the refrigerator, reloaded the gun, and shot four more bullets into Chris before attempting to turn the gun on herself. According to what Kenny told the police, he heard the six shots, and by the time he walked into the room, he saw Vicky shoot twice more for a total of eight bullets fired.

But Chris was shot ten times. When—and where—were the other two shots fired?

I started to formulate another scenario in my mind. Kenny heard six shots because *he* was the shooter. Vicky, who I personally watched sleep through a tornado, could have slept through gunfire until the sound of shots fired in close proximity woke her up. And that's not considering any effects of any drugs she and Chris may have had in their systems, which we can't know because the arresting officers didn't test her blood, nor did the medical examiner perform a toxicity test on Chris' body.

In the scenario I think happened, Vicky slowly wakes up after hearing multiple gunshots, runs into the living room, and sees Kenny standing over Chris with the gun. She panics. Kenny either threatens to kill her and/or himself. She talks him out of it by saying she will take the blame. She walks to the kitchen, reloads the gun, and shoots more rounds into Chris to get gunshot residue on her hands. She calls 911 and confesses. That's what my gut and every cop instinct in my bones say happened. I needed to see the official police report.

I made a Missouri Sunshine Law (similar to a Federal Freedom of Information Act) request to the Stoddard County Sheriff's Department to view the records associated with Vicky's case. They sent me back a letter stating they didn't have to provide me with any information. I filed a complaint with the Missouri Attorney General's office. The investigator from the AG's office agreed the Sheriff's office was in violation of the Sunshine Law. The Sheriff's office complied, but just barely, and sent me a highly redacted report with several pages missing. I knew I had to keep fighting for the truth to come out, no matter how long it would take.

It became obvious that Kenny's mental illness, regardless of whether he believed the doctors or not, was something I had to deal with. Kenny was approved for Social Security in the fall of 2013 and began receiving a monthly check and Medicaid. Now that he had a steady source of money his calls became infrequent and his behavior changed. The first week of January 2014, he called me at midnight, screaming that someone was trying to kill him. I called the Poplar Bluff Police, who found him intoxicated at his apartment but otherwise unharmed. Then on January 11th Kenny entered a convenience store on the east side of Poplar Bluff, across from Mom's old house. He took a beer out of the cooler, began drinking it, and then walked out without paying for it. The clerk chased and confronted him, knocking the beer out of his hand. Kenny ran toward Mom's old house where the police picked him up. The clerk described him as disoriented and clumsy. The Poplar Bluff officers showed Kenny the compassion that well-trained officers pride themselves on; instead of arresting him, they took Kenny to the local hospital where he was admitted to the psychiatric ward for evaluation. They issued him a summons to appear in court at a later date to deal with the actual incident.

Kenny called us from the psychiatric ward and claimed his tea was spiked with something. I called the police and spoke with the Lieutenant who took Kenny to the hospital. He said that Kenny was talking incoherently when they picked him up and was talking about aliens coming after him. The Lieutenant feared for Kenny's safety. The Lieutenant also informed me that Kenny had called them a month earlier to report $635 missing from his wallet. Kenny claimed that he had accidentally dropped his wallet at the grocery store and that two men picked it up and took the money out of it, then threw the wallet back down. It sounded like an impossible story that something like that would happen in a crowded grocery store. I was furious and worried all at the same time. I talked to Jimmy about the arrest.

"How many lies can he get caught in?" asked Jimmy.

"It isn't all his fault. He is probably off his medicine," I replied.

"I wish Vicky and him would just tell the truth. Vicky would be home, and Kenny would be in a mental institution where he can get some help," Jimmy said.

But Kenny's legal troubles had just begun. The probate courts were still in the process of allocating Chris and Vicky's shared property. The trailer, with the mortgage paid by the bank's insurance, could be sold. Even in jail, Vicky retained ownership of her Park Avenue and the two trucks with the outstanding loans. We got the Park Avenue and one truck back from the Isaacs, but the other, older green truck was never located. Kenny claimed he didn't know where it was, but the Isaacs wanted it.

While we were trying to get Kenny back on his medicine and in therapy, Cletus located the missing truck. It had been sold to a man who lived in Wappapello, Missouri. The man told Cletus he purchased it from Kenny, who had signed the title. None of this was legal and we would have tried to work it out, but Cletus ran back to the prosecutor's office. The Isaacs filed a criminal theft by fraud complaint, and on March 24, 2014, Stoddard County Prosecutor Russ Oliver issued a warrant for Kenny's arrest. We were unaware of the warrant, as Kenny was living in Butler County. (Outstanding arrest warrants only become known if the police search your name and Social Security number, or if you've received a summons.)

For the next few months, we continued to work with Kenny to get him to a doctor or to an in-patient hospital. He stopped going to therapy and taking his medicines. He fought our help. I couldn't forcibly commit him to a psychiatric facility nor could I monitor his medicines and appointments from my home in St.

Louis. I applied for conservatorship of his Social Security check, which would have allowed me to ensure his rent and utilities were paid, but he refused. Social Security rightly maintains that a court must determine if someone is unable to care for themself, even with a diagnosis of schizophrenia. The disease itself doesn't prevent a person from living a meaningful life, but Kenny was in the throes of unmedicated and unmanaged mania. We would need to obtain legal guardianship of Kenny as an adult in need to make any financial and medical decisions for him.

That spring was unrelenting with more bad news. My son Julian was diagnosed with Type 1 diabetes. This is a death sentence in our family. Diabetes had afflicted everyone on Mom's side of the family for the last one hundred years. None of the women live past 75. My grandmother died in 1983 at the age of 67 from congestive heart failure caused by diabetes complications. I have it and fight diabetes every single day of my life.

Jimmy and I were tired. It was nearing the end of the school year and I would have liked to give my full attention to my students, but trying to oversee Vicky's case and get Kenny psychiatric help drained me. Jimmy worked and assisted Julian with his medical appointments and medicines. One night as we lay in bed talking about our struggles, Jimmy asked me, "Is there a place where you have been truly happy?" I think he just wanted to ponder a question, but out of nowhere, Seattle popped into my mind.

"Yes, Seattle."

I lived in Seattle in the early 1990s as a young woman in love with grunge music, then moved back to Missouri, where I met Jimmy.

"Let's move there," he said.

"How about we go visit first?"

The more I thought about the idea, the more I wanted to move back to the Pacific Northwest. I wanted to rebuild our lives to reflect who we are and not based on the memory of my criminally inclined relatives. I was torn though—I needed to take care of Vicky and Kenny, I made that promise to Mom. It didn't feel like I was doing a very good job of taking care of anybody, including myself, at the moment. Still, the idea of leaving Missouri took root in my mind. Just to think of leaving and putting all these people and their problems behind me became my favorite daydream.

In mid-July, a lady I knew in Poplar Bluff contacted me on social media. She said she saw Kenny sitting on the side of the road on Main Street. She recognized him from my pictures and asked him if he was my nephew. He told her, "I think so," and started running down the street. She said he left a bag with his computer and clothes on the side of the road. I asked her to hold on to the bag until I could come to get it. It was the first confirmed sighting we had of Kenny in over three months. The phone we had gotten for him no longer worked. He'd been evicted and we had no idea where he was living.

Weeks later, on August 7th, Kenny was arrested by Poplar Bluff Police Department. They stopped him for a routine pedestrian check because he was out walking late at night. And after checking his name in their data system, they saw the outstanding warrant from Stoddard County. He was booked into the Butler County Jail while he awaited extradition to Stoddard County. I answered the collect call from jail, like so many times before.

"Aunt Betty, I got arrested," Kenny said.

"For what?" I thought it was another shoplifting charge.

"No, the old green truck. The Isaacs said I stole it and sold it."

"Did you?"

"No. I haven't seen a green truck."

"Okay. What is your bond?"

"$5,000 or 10%, but you can't pay it until I go to Stoddard County."

"Okay, Jimmy and I will find the money."

Kenny was transferred to Stoddard County, and we bailed him out two days later. However, the Stoddard County prosecutor's office wasn't done with Kenny. For Kenny, it was the start of his descent into a prison of his mind.

On August 9, 2014, the same day we got Kenny out of Stoddard County Jail, Michael Brown Jr., an 18-year-old Black man, was fatally shot by police officer Darren Wilson in Ferguson, Missouri. The shooting occurred a short distance from the Northwest Academy of Law, where I taught criminal justice. The school year would be starting soon, and the always forward-thinking Principal Carter-Thomas had a meeting with the teachers. We could not ignore what was happening in the community and the pain students were feeling. She wanted us to help the young adults channel their feelings into learning how they could improve their communities. I changed my lesson plans to focus on the legalities of due process and what that means in the law's eyes. It was all the more personal to me because, unlike other law enforcement professionals Black students encountered, I was experiencing both sides of the legal system. They knew my family was dealing with the same court system deciding my sister's fate that would decide if Darren Wilson would be indicted for shooting Mike Brown. I knew better than anyone how slowly the wheels of justice turn, and I wanted my students to understand every part of the process.

CHAPTER SIX

As a child, I loved stories, and having a family full of storytellers, those were some of my favorite happy memories. Uncle Jim weaving a tall tale of how he fought Bigfoot in the backwoods, or Mom's convincing recollection of lights from a possible spaceship over the gravel road on her way from work, would spark my imagination. Because Mom had anointed me the "smart one," every night one of my older sisters would read me a Little Golden Book or tell me a fairytale.

The age difference between my older siblings and me left me alone with an imaginary world as my best friend. Playing dress-up was a favorite pastime. I learned from my family—each of them could shift personalities as quickly as a gifted actor. Mom could change her speech pattern and mannerisms with every clothing change. She could drop her deep country accent and instantly sound middle-class and professional when she was wanting something from someone. Grandma Roxie, who was normally an introvert who only socialized with family, became "funeral Roxie," who wore wigs and short dresses to people's funerals. For all her church-going and Bible quoting, there was something about a funeral that uncorked her malice. Instead of paying kind respects, she would spread backhanded compliments like "Charlie was a good old man—too bad he was a drunk." It goes on and on, to the most extreme example of my cousin, James, who faked his death and lived as a completely different person for years.

I learned to be a chameleon—changing with every circumstance. The ability to think on my feet and stay in character is a useful skill in my criminal justice work. Yet, I had also worked hard, and had been blessed by luck to take advantage of opportunities to escape the pull of dead-end jobs and hopelessness faced by so many stuck in a cycle of poverty and mental illness. Like Vicky. Like Kenny. Dropping your accent doesn't help you if there's no future but a fairytale and a handful of painkillers.

Kenny told me over the phone that his bail bondsman, Devin Miller, would drive him to Poplar Bluff. Kenny said he had an apartment and that he would call to let us know he made it there safely.

At home in St. Louis, I looked up Kenny's case online. I should have been keeping regular tabs on him in the Missouri circuit court online public access system. I discovered his landlord filed eviction papers because Kenny hadn't paid his rent in months. I was furious. We were suspicious Kenny wasn't paying his bills. We didn't know where or what he spent his check on. He wasn't a child, and he wasn't deemed incapacitated, so once he received his monthly Social Security check, he was free to spend it as he pleased.

I contacted his landlord to find out how much he owed. I asked him, if I paid Kenny's back rent plus court fees, would he stop the eviction process?

"Yes. When you and your husband were paying, the rent was never late. I have to make a living for myself. I know about his mother murdering that man, and he has problems. But there is only so much I can do," the landlord said. He was as caught up in Kenny's lies as we were.

"I totally understand. I'll wire you the money to get him paid up. Will you stop the eviction process?" I asked.

"Of course. All I want is my money," he said.

As Vicky's case wound through the courts, we didn't want Kenny alone on the streets. We knew he needed stability and couldn't be homeless again, which meant we had to pay for everything. I didn't know if uprooting him from the only area he has ever known would harm his mental health. I wired $700 to the landlord for the three months of back rent and his attorney's fees.

A couple hours later, I contacted Devin the bondsman, who said he didn't drive Kenny to his apartment, but that Kenny took a cab from the jail in Bloomfield, Missouri, to a hotel room in Poplar Bluff. Kenny told him he needed to relax in the hot tub.

I called the hotel and asked for Kenny's room. The clerk

told me he was not there. I described him to the clerk—his very distinctive neck tattoo was the giveaway. She said, "Oh. Mr. August McDougal. He is in Room 321." This was the first time I heard the name August McDougal. But it wouldn't be the last.

"He told us he lost his passport on the plane from Europe. Poor thing. Bless his heart," she said.

I detested when someone would say "bless your heart." For me, it was said as a show of pity or contempt—like when the lunch lady realized you were on "free lunch" or when a teacher asked what you got for your birthday and you had to answer "nothing."

I asked to be put through to his room.

"Hallo," Kenny said in a weird accent—not his familiar Missouri accent but a cross between English and Irish but really neither of them.

"Kenny, I need to talk to you about your apartment," I said.

Someone started knocking on the hotel door.

"'Old on," Kenny said as if he was a business placing me on hold.

"Pizza for August McDougal. Are you Mr. McDougal?" said an unfamiliar male voice.

"Yes, why yes, I am," Kenny said, still using an accent. I heard him pay the delivery person and come back to the phone.

"Hallo."

"Kenny, why are you talking like someone from Belfast, Ireland?"

"You know nothing of Belfast," he said and hung up.

I tried calling again, but he wouldn't answer the motel phone. I requested a wellness check from the Poplar Bluff Police Department, and a few hours later, they called back, saying he was intoxicated and trying to sleep. No accents. No "August McDougal," just a drunk Kenny Smith.

The next day, I called Kenny. He seemed himself, joking with me on the phone.

"Kenny, why haven't you paid your rent in three months?"

"Oh, that was just a misunderstanding. I'll take care of it."

"I took care of it. I paid $700 to your landlord. Now get out of that hotel and go home." The frustration was coming out of me.

"Oh, okay. I'm on my way after I eat."

"If you can't take care of your business, I am gonna file for guardianship and conservatorship of your check. Do you understand?"

"Yes, it is just misunderstandings, like with the old green truck I was supposed to have stolen." With Kenny, it was always someone else's fault.

Kenny settled into his apartment, and we worked out how he would pay us back the rent money. He seemed to be stable and on track and getting himself taken care of. I turned my focus back to Vicky.

I waited all weekend long for Vicky to call me. No call. On Monday, I sent the jail administrator an email. She responded by saying Vicky lost phone privileges for two weeks for arguing with a corrections officer about her medication. This jail administrator showed compassion for her inmates. I advised her of Vicky's conduct disorder and other intellectual disabilities. The jail was gracious in dealing with Vicky, but there comes a time when she had to lose privileges. I had a duty to make sure Vicky was safe, but on the other hand, the rules must be followed.

Missouri is like many states that have challenges managing their rural county jails. The smaller counties, with depressed economies and without a thriving tax base to support their sheriff's departments, have difficulty keeping personnel on staff. The pay is often low—some counties pay only minimum wage for jail positions—and most have only the minimum education requirements of a high school diploma or GED. These officers are expected to keep citizens safe, be mental health aides, and protect prisoners from each other. It's a lot to ask from someone earning very little money, who usually comes from the same communities as the people in the jails.

There are too many documented cases of a low-paid jailer succumbing to the temptation of easy money from corruption.

In a jail environment, temptation comes from all directions, from taking kickbacks from criminal activity in the jails to outright extortion and harassment. The power given to individuals can be easily abused. Correctional officers, like police officers, have a lot of discretion. It takes a disciplined system with firm leadership to keep everyone safe. And when unqualified and untrained people are in positions of power, it sets up a dangerous situation for everyone in a facility.

A few weeks later, I finally spoke to Vicky on the phone. I needed to try to sort out what happened with Kenny's arrest and the old green truck.

"Kenny got arrested," I said.

"What? What for?" she said.

"The Isaacs found the old green truck at some guy's house and filed a complaint with the prosecutor's office. They charged him with stealing. We had to bail him out. Did you know Kenny sold the truck?"

"Yes, I told him to. It was a day or two after the murder, and he needed money."

"You need to contact his public defender and write out a statement."

If this was true, how could the Stoddard County prosecutor charge Kenny with stealing something that Vicky legally owned? But at the same time, if Vicky didn't have the title properly signed over and the papers authorizing Kenny to sell it, and if Kenny illegally signed the title, then in the eyes of the law, the situation was exactly as it appeared: Kenny sold a vehicle he didn't own.

After the "August McDougal" incident in September, Kenny called us at least once a day. Then the calls suddenly stopped. I called his psychiatrist, who would not talk to me because Kenny refused to sign a HIPAA release form. It was back to the same series of lies and schizophrenia-induced bad decisions. And again the rent wasn't paid but this time the landlord called me. I was done. He told me that the apartment was already cleared out, and Kenny was long gone. Phone calls to his cell phone and messages to his doctor and psychiatrist's office were unreturned.

I knew he was not well, and it was tearing me up inside. As frustrated and angry as I was, I knew Kenny was fundamentally sick. I didn't sleep the rest of the week and when it was finally the weekend, we drove to Poplar Bluff to look for Kenny. We went up and down the streets, searching for anyone who might know where he might be. We got lucky after a few hours: as we rounded the corner on Kinzer Street, I saw him walking in front of the local radio station. He looked tired and had a black eye, the left side of his face was swollen, and his lip was busted open like it had been punched. I pulled the car over and stopped in front of him.

"Kenny, are you okay?" I asked.

He did not answer.

I asked again, "Kenny, are you okay?"

He looked at me.

"Kenny, can you hear me?"

"Yeah, yeah. I can hear you," he answered. As he walked closer, he smelled like he hadn't had a bath in days.

"Let's get you something to eat."

We went to a buffet-style restaurant and sat in the back of the restaurant. Kenny ate ten full plates of food. I asked him where his clothes and other belongings were. He shrugged. After we finished eating, we went to Walmart and bought him two pairs of pants, two new shirts, a package of socks and underwear, and brand-new shoes. I told Kenny he'd have to come up and stay with us, and he said that was fine.

He did not speak a single word during the three-hour drive back to St. Louis, just gazed out the window. He took a shower and fell asleep on the couch as soon as we got home, then slept for 14½ hours.

When he woke up, I asked Kenny, "Have you been going to therapy?"

"I don't remember."

"Have you been taking your medication?"

Bridge over the Black River

"I don't remember," he said.

Thanksgiving holiday was only a few weeks away. I wanted Kenny safe with us. If we could get him back on his medication and in therapy, maybe he would stabilize, and he could live on his own in Poplar Bluff. He wouldn't help us help him. He wouldn't tell us what happened and how he got beat up. I finally had our local hospital contact his doctor to, at the very least, get his prescriptions transferred and filled. Of course, people deserve privacy, and medical history should be confidential. Still, it should have been evident to everyone from doctors to law enforcement that Kenny was mentally ill and we were his family desperately trying to help him. Especially as it became apparent he couldn't help himself.

113

CHAPTER SEVEN

Poplar Bluff's most famous former resident was Linda Bloodworth-Thomason, the creator of the 1990s television program *Designing Women*. The main character, Julia Sugarbaker, was the stereotype of the genteel Southern lady, who in an episode shared the old Southern truism that in our families, "We were proud of our crazy people and we didn't hide them away." That sentiment may have been true of the wealthy Faulkner-esque South of the early 20th century, but it wasn't how poor people in southern Missouri dealt with mental illness. And it sure as hell wasn't how my family dealt with problems.

As a child, I understood Mom didn't act like the other moms I saw on television or even like my namesake, Mayor Betty Absheer. I wanted a Mom who behaved correctly, that I didn't have to feel embarrassed by or ashamed of. I wanted a calm, peaceful life with clean clothes and a refrigerator full of food. Every school day at 2:45 p.m., my arms and legs started shaking because class was getting out soon, and I didn't know who I was coming home to. Maybe it was nice Mom who would have something cooked and talked nice to me, or perhaps it was screaming raging Mom just looking for a reason to hit me.

This type of chaos can be addictive. There's a law enforcement concept called the Locard Principle that says a person can't go into a crime scene without leaving something behind and can't exit a crime scene without taking something with them. It generally applies to physical evidence, but I've always thought the idea can apply to psychological places as well. Living in a family with constant stress and chaos created a deeply rooted need for drama in my life; it was only when everything was disordered did I feel normal. I often found myself seeking chaos—and trying to bring order to it; maybe that's one reason I was drawn to police work. If it wasn't for my faith and having a few examples like my favorite teacher, Mrs. Kingery, or Trixie's mother-in-law Edna Hastings, I

115

wouldn't have found a way to quiet the noise in my head and find a sense of calm.

I could finally sleep without the fear of something happening to Kenny now that he was under my roof. We took precautions. There were no firearms in my house. All the sharp objects were put away at night. I am a light sleeper, so if he woke up, we could hear him coming up the stairs. We settled into a routine: every morning, I fixed breakfast, went to work, came home, made dinner, and watched television with everyone. Once he was back on his medication and had a daily routine to follow, Kenny was pleasant and stable as he filled his days watching television or listening to music on the computer. He took daily showers and groomed himself. He even picked up after himself. It was a vast improvement from the man we picked up off the streets of Poplar Bluff.

Sustaining any kind of relationship with Kenny remained difficult. Kenny's narcissistic personality disorder meant that he dictated most of the conversations. Not only did we have to be careful what we said to Kenny, but, although he was taking his medications, his combination of schizophrenia and newly diagnosed PTSD combined with the narcissistic personality disorder also meant that he was easily triggered into manic episodes. He had no interest in us or what we did and only wanted to talk about professional wrestling and his memories of my Mom or things that happened before her death, which were probably, all things considered, the happiest time of his life. I instructed my family not to bring up the murder but let him talk and listen quietly if Kenny did.

A letter from Kenny's public defender interrupted this month of peace. His attorney wrote that Kenny's theft case was granted a venue change to Cape Girardeau, Missouri. Cape Girardeau was a university town, and we hoped the jury pool would be a little bit more educated, tolerant, and compassionate toward people suffering from mental illness. The letter triggered a new manic episode in Kenny. He began to spend all his time uselessly researching his case on the internet. He would pace up and down the hallway for hours. We would hear him talking to himself about the charges in the middle of the night and making endless notes to himself.

The episodes increased until he suffered a full psychotic break a few days later. Kenny's eyes looked forward and widened; his breath became shallow out of his open mouth. His mind became trapped in some dark place, a place where we, no matter how much love and compassion we gave him, could not gain entrance.

I called his public defender and left several messages that went unanswered. Kenny was in no condition to go to trial. Especially for a crime that wasn't really a crime but part of a convoluted paperwork vendetta. The lawyers, either Kenny's public defender or Stoddard County's prosecutor, just needed Vicky to swear out a statement that she asked Kenny to sell the truck on her behalf. I tried to talk to him about the situation.

"Kenny, let's talk about the old green truck," I said in an effort to discover what was happening with him. I could see his hand start to form one of his bird calls.

"Okay," he said.

"What do you remember about the sale of that truck?"

"To be quite honest, I don't really remember. I racked my brain about it." His hands shook more now.

"You don't even remember selling this truck?"

"Mother said she told me to sell it right after they took her to jail. The prosecutor said I signed the title, but I don't remember."

"What do you remember about that day?"

"Nothing... I think they want to send me to jail. The Isaacs have got the prosecutor in their hands, and he's an elected puppet. They're just playing him to make me suffer," he said, sitting on his hands to control the shaking.

"Do you need your medicine?" I asked.

"I already took it. This is just old Firewood doing the bird calls," he laughed.

"Kenny, you said they diagnosed you after Mom died. How did they diagnose you?" I asked.

"Well, I was eating at the Mexican restaurant in Dexter when my heart started hurting. I walked outside and thought I was

117

having a heart attack. I passed out and died. These people had been talking to me, and somehow I woke up in the hospital a couple days later," he said.

"I am confused. I thought that is when they told you were schizophrenic?"

"I heard some people talking to me. They talk to me sometimes. You know, usually, it's nonsense, but I guess I listened to them and passed out."

I tried to read between the lines. It sounded like he was having an anxiety attack because of the voices in his head. He did something and ended up in the hospital. Since he was talking, I kept asking questions.

"Who are these people that talk to you?"

"Some people here, some people there. No one you would know, and then there is a mean son of a bitch, Hobo Jackson. He would rather kill you than look at you. He doesn't like you. You know too much."

"Do I know Hobo Jackson? Is it someone I arrested?"

"No, you ain't smart enough to catch Hobo Jackson." Kenny laughed. "No one is or ever will be."

We kept Kenny as calm as possible and occupied with tasks to help keep him from spinning into another manic episode. The Isaacs and the Stoddard County prosecutor's office didn't care how much mental anguish this trumped-up charge inflicted on Kenny's already fragile psyche. That was more of a crime than selling Vicky and Chris' broken-down truck that didn't even have a motor. At least with Kenny living with us, we could work with his doctors to handle his issues. Vicky's trial date was getting closer, and she too was becoming more unstable. I now dreaded her weekend calls.

One week she called in a panic over her blanket. The next week she complained of having an allergic reaction after being bitten by bed bugs. Then she said she was tasered by guards for requesting another blanket. I know that she could be defiant, but she had an implanted artery stent from the 2012 stroke, and getting a jolt of electrical charge from a taser could trigger a heart attack and kill her. I emailed the jail administrator to ask her what was happening. They claimed to have no complaints and that the linens are sent out for weekly sanitization and pest treatment. I requested that doctors examine her, and they confirmed she had a bruised rib. I asked her new public defender lawyer, Ms. Tucka, to check on her.

Patti Tucka was a no-nonsense lawyer who worked with the public defender's office. She was the fifth public defender assigned to Vicky's case. She wasn't fresh from law school, but an experienced litigator who specialized in insurance law before joining the public defender's office. She called often to get background about Vicky and details about the case.

"I wanted to speak with you, Ms. Frizzell, about the gun used in the murder. There are the initials M.P. scratched into it and no serial number. Whose gun is this?" she asked.

I gave Ms. Tucka the straightest answer I could: "It was Mom's gun. Her name was Mary Pickard—M.P. were her initials. I didn't know the numbers were scratched off. The last time I saw that gun was in 1997 when Mom used it to practice shooting with me when I was going through the police academy. Vicky and Kenny got all of Mom's things in her will after her death in 2001 and had Mom's gun. The will is on file at the Butler County courthouse," I told her.

Mom had guns around the house for as long as I could remember. She taught us to appreciate guns—don't fear them but respect them. They are not toys. Children from southeast Missouri owned guns before they owned dolls and toy cars. Long before school shootings made the news, the boys drove to high school with guns in racks mounted behind the seat. Schools weren't in session during the two-week deer hunting season. Hunter education and gun safety were taught to everyone in the eighth grade.

Almost every woman I knew in Poplar Bluff during the '70s and '80s had a gun. Mom was an avid hunter, a card-carrying

NRA member until the day she died. She didn't hunt for sport but for food. She didn't have an armory, just a few good ones that would help a five-year-old go to bed with a full stomach. They were a necessary tool with a purpose: like a washing machine washes clothes, a gun was used to gather food.

In 1976, Mom's last husband, Aubrey, died and our house was crowded and chaotic. My two older sisters still lived at home. We lived in a trailer on ten acres in the country outside of Poplar Bluff. There was never enough of anything—especially food. Mom refused to apply for government assistance, saying it was for "other people" and she wouldn't sign up for welfare as long as she was able to work. But there weren't too many employers in rural Missouri looking to hire a newly widowed mother of eight.

We lived off the land. Vegetables grew from a small garden, a few chickens we raised, wild plants foraged in the woods, and animals we hunted and snared. Vicky and I would pick wild green onions, and Mom fried potatoes or made pancakes for breakfast. We skipped lunch or sometimes had a bologna sandwich, and more fried potatoes and a little chicken or hamburger meat for dinner. Sometimes Vicky made me ketchup and crackers. A big treat was after church on Sundays when Mom killed and fried a chicken for lunch.

When I was five and Vicky was eleven years old, we marched out into the woods with Mom's gun in hand as Vicky led me on my first hunting expedition. Our mission was to find something else to eat besides eggs and fried potatoes. While city girls my age were safe in their warm houses playing with Barbie dolls or having tea parties, I had an old .410 shotgun and a box of shells. I didn't play dress-up with pearls and high heels; I wore Mom's oversized orange jacket and thick rubber boots as we trudged deeper into the woods behind our trailer.

The cold December wind hurt almost as much as the hunger in my stomach. My teenage sisters were too good to go out looking for food. Vicky loved to go hunting. Being in the woods was one of the places that gave her any peace—with the wind blowing through the trees and the animal sounds only she knew and not

Mom yelling how stupid she was. When Vicky fished our dinner out of the pond or shot a rabbit she became Wonder Woman, the heroine who saved us from fried potatoes.

As we reached the tree line, Vicky, in all her hard-won hunting wisdom, had last-minute instructions.

"Did you load your gun?" she asked.

"Yes," I said.

Of course, I knew how to load a gun. I couldn't count the times I watched Mom load her gun to shoot squirrels off the back porch.

"Are you sure how to pull the trigger without jerking it?" she asked.

"Yes." I was tired of her questions. My stomach ached from hunger.

"I am going to the gravel pit to look for rabbits. You can stay out here but don't go any further than the Johnsons' fence. You understand?" she said, more like a mother than an older sister.

"Yes," I replied.

"Remember, point at what you're gonna shoot and look only at the front sight. And don't shoot yourself. If you hear a gunshot, meet me back at the chicken coop."

"Yes."

"Are you going to be okay? Don't do anything stupid because I'll be the one Mom beats," she said. She didn't have to remind me who would be in trouble.

"Yes. I am fine."

She walked away, trudging the few patches of wet unfrozen red Missouri clay dirt. I wrapped my short, chubby fingers around the stock of the gun. After a few minutes of sitting perfectly still, I saw my prey, a little brown rabbit hopping softly on the light snow-covered ground.

My heart pounded in my ears. I lowered the gun. The rabbit continued to move closer to me. Mom taught us to shoot small animals, like squirrels, rabbits, and turkeys, in the head—that way, it preserves the meat. I looked in its big dark eyes and slowly squeezed the trigger. At the sound of the shot being ejected from the barrel, the rabbit ran off, and I fell on my back. Vicky ran over

121

to check and laughed. I eventually became a better shot, but fried potatoes never tasted so good on that cold December day.

I knew Vicky knew how to use a gun. She was a skilled hunter. There was no need for the excessive number of shots fired at Chris. Even if I accept the idea that she wanted to kill him, she could have done it with a single shot; I'd even allow that she might have emptied the entire six rounds, but there was no reason to reload and shoot four more. Given that they weren't fighting that morning or even the day before, what reason was there for her to harm Chris? A forensic investigator will tell you: when a killer shoots someone that many times, the shooter is filled with rage. Chris' killer had a personal score to settle. The killer wouldn't be someone with a personality like Vicky's who expected and absorbed abuse, but someone like Kenny whose mental illness and personality wouldn't allow for the disrespect of Chris blacking his eye the previous week to stand unanswered.

Kenny's descent into psychosis continued. He had difficulty distinguishing between the reality of our home and the world in his head. At first, my family didn't tell me how disconnected Kenny was becoming because the episodes were short and occurred while I was at work. Eventually, his odd behavior carried over into the evening hours. Kenny's thoughts grew more unorganized and scattered. We called his psychiatrist, who suggested we bring him in, but the soonest appointment was over two weeks away after the Thanksgiving holiday.

On November 24th, St. Louis County Prosecutor Bob McCulloch was going to announce the grand jury findings of the evidence presented against Officer Darren Wilson for the killing of Michael Brown, whose death at police hands gave rise to the Black Lives Matter movement. We were glued to the TV watching live news coverage as McCulloch announced he wasn't charging Wilson with the shooting of Michael Brown. It was the start of the unrest as the television broadcast images of angry and anguished people marching in protest. And as tempers flared, we saw a police car set afire and windows of surrounding buildings getting busted out. I could see Kenny grow angry.

He began talking to himself in a quiet, low voice. His jaw was clenched. He jumped up, pointed his finger at the television screen, made a karate chop motion with both arms, and pushed away from the chair. He said, "Die, every single one of them. One by Goddamn one by Goddamn one of them." He did it again. And again. The fourth time he got up, he stuck his left hand out like he was shooting a gun. "Die by die by die every last one of them," he said and sat back down. He began quietly rocking back and forth.

I could only imagine how he coped with the delusions, the trauma triggers, and stress while living in Vicky and Chris' dysfunctional home. Anything could have set him off. A fistfight with Chris would have been something that might have pushed Kenny into psychosis. Was it really Kenny, or "Hobo Jackson," the manifestation of his delusion, acting out so violently toward the television images? Was seeing the violence projected causing him to remember the violence that led to Chris' death and Vicky's incarceration?

Kenny fell asleep in the chair as he rocked back and forth to unconsciously soothe himself. I didn't want to disturb his sleep. I went to bed but couldn't get my suspicions out of my mind. A real murderer could be downstairs with my family, and my sister could be sitting in a jail cell, lying to protect her son.

The next morning my husband and I sat at the kitchen table and heard Kenny talking to himself in the next room. Kenny walked into the kitchen.

"Do you want me to make you something for breakfast?" I asked.

"I don't want a goddamn thing. If I want something, I will tell you," Kenny said.

"Okay. Did you take your medicine?" I asked.

"Don't you worry about if I took my medicine or not," he said, walking back into the living room.

123

I didn't engage with Kenny in case he was on the tipping point of having an episode. He seemed so angry and on edge. Kenny yelled from the other room. Jimmy and I ran into the front room. Kenny stood over his shoes, yelling at his right shoe.

"You no-good son of a bitch. I am getting my $50,000 from you today," Kenny said, pointing his finger at the shoe.

"Kenny, Kenny, what is happening?" Jimmy asked.

"Give me my goddamn money," Kenny said, placing both his hands around the shoe as if he was putting them on someone's neck and strangling it.

"How you like that. How do you like that? Die, you son of a bitch. Die," he said, gripping the shoe in a stranglehold.

"Kenny, stop. What are you doing?" I asked.

He stopped shaking the shoe and looked at me. He took one hand off and pointed his finger at me.

"Shut up bitch, or you are next," he said, shaking his finger at me.

"Kenny, do you need your medicine?" I asked.

He walked up to me and looked down at me menacingly. I prepared to punch him if needed.

"You know, don't you. You always knew. You knew... you know too much," he said.

"I know what, Kenny? I know what? Tell me what I know."

"You can't prove a damn thing. You know too much," he said with a mocking smile.

"You may have fooled them fools in southeast Missouri... or my poor sick sister... but you don't fool me. I know. I have always known. You killed Chris." I finally said what had been in my head for the past seven months out loud to him.

He stumbled backward as if my words hit him in the stomach. Kenny looked at Jimmy and then back at me. My words hung in the silence between us. He tried to compose himself and take control of the situation.

"I need my $50,000, so shut the hell up," he replied.

Jimmy pulled me back into the kitchen.

"He needs to go to the hospital. He's getting violent," Jimmy said.

"Do you want me to call the police?"

"No, I can get him to go," Jimmy said.

We walked back into the front room.

"Kenny, let's go talk to a doctor. He might know where your money is," Jimmy said.

"Now, finally, someone is making some damn sense around here," Kenny said, putting his shoes on.

Jimmy grabbed his keys from the table.

"Let's go," Jimmy said.

Kenny got up and put his finger in my face.

"They better have my money, bitch."

"Come on, Kenny," Jimmy said, opening the door.

Jimmy drove to the psychiatric hospital that was less than three miles from our house.

This was the closest I got to a confession from him. The truth was buried somewhere deeper in the darkness of his quickly collapsing mind.

It was ludicrous for me even to think of telling the Stoddard County Sheriff's Department of my suspicions. For Vicky to be free, she would have to tell the truth and Kenny would have to clearly confess to killing Chris. The Sheriff's Department had closed their murder investigation and Vicky was going to stand trial. Why should they do anything else?

There was no real physical evidence in the case. Vicky said that the Sheriff told her that her DNA was on the gun, and she tested positive for gunshot residue, and Kenny did not. But an officer trying to get a confession out of someone isn't obligated to tell the truth. I needed to see the police and lab reports for myself. The immediate aftermath of something so traumatic as a shooting leads people to do unthinkable things. False confessions happen more often than people may realize. I'm convinced that Vicky took the blame for Kenny's actions. Going to jail for her son would be her ultimate motherly sacrifice. It would be the one thing she could finally do for her son to make up for the guilt she felt for years of failing him.

Jimmy called from the psychiatric ward. The doctors wanted to keep Kenny for observation. A few hours later, Julian and I went to the hospital to check on him. The room was empty, except for the hospital bed. Kenny lay on his back, dressed in a hospital nightgown and bright yellow socks on his feet. He wasn't the same angry and agitated person he was when he left the house. But he also wasn't his normal self. He wasn't in his usual smiling and joking mood. He had a severe look on his face as he put his arms behind his head and began talking again about the $50,000 that someone gave someone else in Poplar Bluff to kill someone. I felt it was better to keep him talking as we weren't sure if this was still an episode or something else. I asked him, "What organization gave you $50,000 to kill someone?"

"Not me but someone else. But not me. They do it all the time. To perform or issue a hit."

"Then what happened?"

"Things behind the scenes. The courtroom is not how things are done. You should know that by now."

"Who is this unknown organization?"

"I refuse to say."

"Why? Did they threaten you?"

"I don't know nothing. They say, 'Ain't you enjoy your booze.' I said, 'Of course, I am good.' Why would I say anything against them? Hell, I am enjoying myself."

"How did you get hooked up with them?

"What can I say? Shit happens. I got hooked up with them a long time ago—way before you'll even know. Hey, guess what? They are the people… it doesn't even matter about them. They ain't gonna do nothing to them anyway."

The hospital kept him in observation for two days. Kenny was released with his medication and came back to our house. He appeared more like himself and explained he was tired and needed a break.

But that didn't erase what happened. It didn't make the threats and what Kenny said to me just disappear. I couldn't trust Kenny being in my house with my family any longer. As a police officer, I've been cussed out in about every language but never before in my own home. We needed to find Kenny another place to live that was safe for him—but more importantly, safe for us.

I knew in my heart that he shot and killed Chris. A detective must be impartial and shouldn't be swayed by emotions but base their findings on facts. As a trained investigator, I must remain open-minded, logical, and objective. The facts pointed toward Kenny, but I didn't have the evidence in the form of police and lab reports.

As much as I wanted to him to be accountable for what I'm sure he did, there was still the issue of his mental health condition. For a crime to be committed, one had to have both the guilty mind and commit the guilty act. The act was definitely there—Chris was dead, and Kenny probably was the one who did it. But the guilty mind? The state of his mind would absolutely come into question. Was the shooter Kenny as we knew him or one of the "voices" in his head? He had already presented himself to other people as another person—"August McDougal." And who was this "Hobo Jackson" he kept referring to? Was it a real human being or another person from the deep reaches of his mind?

Jimmy and I decided it would be a better idea for him to move back to Poplar Bluff. He was familiar with the town and would be closer to his psychiatrist. He liked the psychiatrist in Poplar Bluff a lot better than the one in St. Louis. When I came home from work a few days later, Kenny said he had found a place to rent on Main Street in Poplar Bluff.

The next day, Jimmy and Kenny took the train to Poplar Bluff, where it became apparent that there was no apartment. Jimmy tried to get Kenny a motel room for the month, but again, as Kenny was an adult we had no legal control over him. Jimmy came home the next morning. For the next few weeks, as Kenny stayed on his medication, he called us to check in daily. We were confident that he could manage his illness with his psychiatrist's help. Yet it soon became apparent that it was only a foolish hope.

127

By week three in Poplar Bluff, Kenny stopped calling. We called the hotel and found out that he didn't pay for the month but for a week. He left all the stuff that we purchased for him in the hotel room. I paid for the hotel to send it back to us. Kenny was once again on the streets.

Vicky still was facing trial and Kenny was the key witness. I called Ms. Tucka to give an update about Kenny's condition and his strange ramblings, and my suspicions about who really pulled the trigger. Although Kenny didn't clearly make a confession, Ms. Tucka also believed the whole story wasn't being told. She knew of Vicky's reluctance to implicate Kenny.

"There is no proof that he did this. But it does give me a basis for questioning him under oath in the deposition," she said.

$\mathcal{T}$hat night I just wanted to be alone. I failed Vicky, and now she might take her last breath in jail. Kenny was running around homeless and unmedicated in Poplar Bluff. What a disappointment I would be for Mom. I went to my room, and hopelessness washed over me.

Women from my part of the country deal with hopelessness in three ways: we turn to food, turn to bad men, or turn to the Lord. Food wasn't helping me; I didn't need any more men—I needed the One who had guided me this far. I strive to be a good person, but I am not a religious person. The atrocities I witnessed in the name of organized religion scared me. I needed strength.

That night in my bedroom, I got on my knees and talked to the Lord.

"Dear Lord, I can't do this anymore. I can't cry any more tears," I said.

In silence, I waited for an answer—any sign—as tears ran down my cheeks. Through the tears, I flashed to a memory of Mom singing along with Patsy Cline: *A closer walk with thee—I am weak, but thou are strong. Jesus keep me from all wrong. I'll be satisfied as long, as I walk, let me walk close to thee.* Then images of Puget Sound and Lake Washington welcoming me came to me. I needed to go back to the Pacific Northwest and find my center.

CHAPTER EIGHT

$\mathcal{D}$isappearing was an art form in my family. Great-Uncle James disappeared after being questioned in a series of deaths. No one in the family ever heard from him again. In 1979, my cousin, also named James, was charged in federal court with a variety of serious firearms violations while also under indictment for burglary. James sold a deputy sheriff, and then later, undercover ATF agents, machine guns and other stolen weapons. He was convicted in absentia of those and additional charges after his car was found in the Black River. Both the authorities and his immediate family concluded that he killed his wife and then committed suicide. However, he was found very much alive several years later in Texas. He was caught and later died in federal prison.

When I was 12, my oldest sister, Jackie, and her two children disappeared from San Diego, California. When she was only a young teenager, Jackie moved to California to live with Mom's sister and her family. I only met Jackie once, when I was four years old. I never knew the real story of why Jackie left. She told Grandma Roxie that our brother raped her. I was told that she was a disciplinary problem but also that she couldn't take living in the house where her brother raped her, and her mother beat her. After a few years, Jackie left our aunt's house and married a much older man who was affiliated with biker gangs in California.

In the summer of 1983, Jackie and the children were supposed to come to Missouri for a visit but never showed up. Mom tried to get the San Diego Police involved, but since Jackie was an adult, they wouldn't even take a police report. Law enforcement is reluctant to get involved in these kinds of family situations because oftentimes an adult is estranged from their family by choice and does not want to be found.

Mom became obsessed with finding Jackie and her kids. I spent years helping Mom look for her. She placed ads in magazines and would call the police whenever she learned of a "Jane Doe" body. This was during the late 1980s, well before the internet connected us to each other whether we liked it or not. It was incredibly time-consuming to search for Jackie, and was another incident in my life that piqued my interest in investigation.

When Mom died in 2001, I still kept looking for them. A friend in the FBI located Jackie in 2003. She was living in Florida, drug-addicted and alcoholic. Her daughter, Alpha, died in 1995 from complications of the flu. Jackie told me that she gave her son Michael to a professor at UCLA. That gave me hope and I called every single professor listed at the college to no avail. I continued to use my spare time and resources to find Michael, against Jackie's wishes. She claimed that he was better off and we shouldn't bother him in his new life, but the truth was worse than I could imagine.

Jackie abandoned Michael at a park when he was only ten years old. He was found hours later and taken to the local police. He had no identification, and Jackie, true to her Frizzell nature, had used a number of false names during his life so that Michael didn't even know his real name or the name of his father. I was lucky that Michael too felt that he needed answers to his early childhood trauma and reached out to the daytime television show host Dr. Phil. You can surely have opinions about the nature of these kinds of shows, but when the show's producers began looking for Jackie, they found me. You can watch the August 10, 2006 episode and read a summary of the events on the *Dr. Phil Show* website.[1] Through the show, I was able to meet Michael and his family. I'm proud to know that he's grown into a fine man despite the abuse and trauma he suffered.

𝕴 needed to get on with my life, so we followed through with our plan to move to Washington state in the summer of 2015. Moving gave me something to hope for besides the constant worry of Vicky and Kenny. I wanted to run away from the whole mess, but duty and love compelled me to continue to advocate for both of them.

---

1 *Dr. Phil Show*, episode 727, August 10, 2006.

Kenny after the murder

Washington is very progressive with respect to health care compared to Missouri. Washington's mental health programs offered more specialized care and a progressive approach to treating schizophrenia and narcissistic personality disorders; it would have meant an entirely new opportunity for Kenny. I wished it hadn't taken us so long to realize how very sick he was. The glimpses of the old Kenny we saw when he took his medication were worth all the trouble of working to obtain conservatorship. This was the final step before making our move to Washington.

But we hadn't heard from Kenny in months. We took turns calling hotels and bars around Poplar Bluff. Our attorney had started the paperwork for the conservatorship hearing, and Kenny would have to be served the legal papers and notified of his court date to move forward. In most conservator cases, the person in need agrees to guardianship or is in a care facility. But now, the paperwork was done, and process servers searched all over Poplar Bluff for Kenny, who proved to be too good at hiding out.

Finishing up the loose ends in Missouri to complete the 1,500-mile move to Seattle was a lot of work. I left my job at the end of the school year, and it hurt to tell my principal I wouldn't be back next year. I loved my students and would miss them tremendously. I would have loved to stay and see them all graduate, but I needed to leave Missouri for my mental and physical health.

For months there were no updates to Kenny's still-pending theft case in Stoddard County. We also didn't know where or how Kenny was living. During our once-a-week phone calls, Vicky would ask if I heard from Kenny, and I would have to tell her no. Our attorney, Mr. Albright, advised us that Kenny's case for conservatorship could proceed if we moved to Seattle, but we would have to come back to Missouri for the hearing. In July 2015, a few weeks before we moved, I made a final attempt to find him and drove down to Poplar Bluff. I put my police skills to work and canvassed the area Kenny frequented, but I could not find him. When somebody doesn't want to be found, they don't want to be found.

We finally decided that there would be no more searching for Kenny. On the last Saturday in August 2015, we packed the car and started the three-day drive west to our new lives. We spent the fall getting acclimated to our new jobs and home, and by Christmas it felt like we had settled into life outside of Seattle.

On January 21, 2016, the judge in Kenny's theft case amended the bond that restricted him to remain in the state of Missouri and ordered him to wear a GPS ankle monitor. It meant that if we could find Kenny, we could proceed with conservatorship and move him to Washington and get better help for him. I contacted his probation officer, hoping she would assist in getting through to Kenny as it was apparent that he was avoiding me. She said she spoke with Kenny, and he claimed that he didn't know who I was. After proving our familial connection, she tried to help but was limited by the law. Our attempts to serve the conservatorship notification papers couldn't be given to Kenny through her office because they hadn't been adjudicated before a judge—but that was the reason we were trying to serve the papers. We were locked in a bureaucratic loop.

A couple months later, the probation officer called me. Apparently, Kenny had cut off his GPS ankle monitor system in early May in downtown Poplar Bluff. Now I was worried about his safety because this was the longest time he had been out of contact with both us and the legal system. On May 11, 2016,

Stoddard County issued an arrest warrant for failure to abide by the probation order.

What a nightmare. No one knew where he was. It wasn't until six months later in November when we got a call from Poplar Bluff bail bondsman Devin Miller, letting us know that he found Kenny! Stoddard County Sheriff's Department arrested Kenny on May 22nd and had held him in custody all this time. The State of Missouri Probation Office hadn't been informed. His public defender hadn't been notified. The county kept a mentally ill man locked in jail for six months without notifying proper authorities or his family.

Kenny finally called me at the prodding of bail bondsman Miller and again, he spoke with a mixture of an English and Irish accent.

"Bettyeee, I am incarcerated in Stoddard County Jail, and the bondsman wants a chat with you to bail me out."

Meanwhile, Vicky's trial date was finally set for December 15, 2016, three and a half years after Chris' killing, and as the case inched closer, she became restless. She wanted the case over. The years in jail began to wear on her.

Vicky's public defender, Ms. Tucka, called to ask if I could get Vicky some new clothes for her trial. Of course I could, but she had lost so much weight that I'd have some difficulty knowing her correct size. To most people going to jail is the most awful thing that can happen, but for someone like Vicky, who lived in constant physical and emotional abuse, the boundaries, routine, and relative safety of jail was a godsend of stability.

Patti Tucka called to interview me one more time. She already had five banker boxes filled with the previous public defenders' notes and Vicky's medical records. But she wanted more. She was the first lawyer who wanted to get a clear picture of who Vicky is and the circumstances of her life before and after she married Chris.

We had set aside a two-hour telephone appointment to go over the materials and let Patti Tucka hear the details hidden for too long. She was matter-of-fact and to the point: "Now, Ms. Frizzell, I am going to ask you some questions. Please feel free to take your time and answer clearly and concisely to the best of your knowledge."

I was ready for the skeletons to fall out of the closet—no more secrets. I told Ms. Tucka everything I knew about Vicky and Chris.

For the first part of their marriage, both were employed as factory workers by Tyson Foods in Dexter, Missouri. Neither of them loved the work; no one enjoys working in a meat processing factory, but Tyson's was one of the largest, and only, employers in the area. The work allowed them to still wrestle on the weekends.

I never thought about Chris' wrestling career as a career, really, but there is a history of wrestlers with chemical dependency and domestic violence issues. In the past decade, the public has learned of the tragic stories of wrestlers like Chris Benoit, who, after years of substance abuse, killed his wife and children and then himself. Wrestling Hall of Fame members Jerry Lawler, Jimmy "Superfly" Snuka, and Scott Hall all have arrests for domestic violence. Other less famous wrestlers have laundry lists of major and minor incidents traced back to a combination of drugs and traumatic brain injuries.

Chris didn't work for a major wrestling company and never got proper medical treatment when he was injured. He wrestled in small, unregulated matches with anything-goes rules that kept the action and violence on edge to keep the fans coming back week after week. Between the days spent training and nights in the ring, Chris suffered repeated blows to the body and head. After matches, Chris often complained of headaches and dizziness. Sometimes, the day after a bout, he wouldn't be able to move himself off the couch or drive a car. He was never evaluated for concussions, let alone something more severe like progressive degenerative brain disease or chronic traumatic encephalopathy (CTE), which can cause confusion, depression, aggression, impulse control problems, and impaired judgment. Chris told me he suffered excruciating pain in his ankle and back from the falls he took as a wrestler. Later in life, Chris became dependent on prescription pills to function with the pain.

Puxico Homecoming

Chris had a problem of not being able to differentiate between the wrestling ring's storylines and real life. Chris' father Donald, the wrestling promoter, hosted a benefit show for kids with heart trouble—except that he kept all the money. A disgruntled wrestler, who had both donated his time and was supposed to get funds for his sick child, confronted Chris and Vicky as they were leaving the annual Puxico High School Homecoming celebration. They had tried to speak to Donald, but he ran away from them. But Chris had expected the confrontation because his brothers had hyped him up to fight for their family and for their father's honor. His family often exploited Chris' bipolar disorder to have him fight their battles.

As Chris and Vicky got in their car, the wrestler and his wife demanded their share of the promised funds. As the situation escalated, the woman jumped on Vicky's back, and the husband jumped on Chris. The police watched the fight for a short time, thinking it was staged as a promotion for an upcoming wrestling show!

135

In 2006, Vicky experienced a couple of job-related injuries and quit. She applied, and was immediately approved, for Social Security disability due to her anxiety issues.

The company outsourced Chris' position to a third-party contractor, and he was let go not long after Vicky quit. He drew unemployment benefits from 2006 to 2009 while he too applied for Social Security disability. He was denied numerous times for reasons I don't know, but was finally approved in 2010.

Their problems really began when Chris got his Social Security and Medicaid. Because he had medical insurance, the doctors gave him opiate painkillers for his chronic work and wrestling injuries. He had already taken painkillers on and off for other injuries, but as we now know, the pharmaceutical industry was encouraging doctors to prescribe a daily dosage of opiates for patients. He began abusing the pills soon after he started taking them. Vicky went to the same doctor and was also given painkillers.

Vicky already had a long history of attaching herself to men who were violent and emotionally cold. Coupled with her propensity for addictive behaviors, it was only a short while before she fell into using pills with Chris. Vicky had some physical injuries during her life, but it was the psychological wounds that were momentarily numbed by painkillers. By 2011 she was using them daily to cope with the stress of daily life. Once opiates had been introduced into their relationship, the violence became more frequent, and they both became more erratic.

How can anyone know someone else's marriage? I knew they were both abusing drugs, but we really didn't see each other. I lived in St. Louis and focused on my family and building my career. We really didn't see each other during those years—a call every week or so. When we came down to Poplar Bluff to visit, Vicky would have to sneak away from Chris to see us because he didn't like my husband, Jimmy. Once, Chris tried to fight Jimmy while the family was at a hotel together. Chris would often get angry and pick fights with people. Even strangers.

Despite Chris' temper, Vicky seemed happy. She seemed to have been accepted and close to the Isaac family. She liked his stepmother, and they did things together until she passed away in 2009. Chris' sister Doris and her husband Cletus were witnesses at Chris and Vicky's wedding. Vicky loved spending time with her nieces and nephews. She bought the kids things at yard sales and flea markets.

Chris' uncontrollable rage seemed to increase in the last year. On a visit to Poplar Bluff, Jimmy, Julian, and I visited a hotel and invited Vicky, Chris, and Kenny to join us as a "mini-vacation." While Jimmy, Julian, and Kenny enjoyed swimming and relaxing in the pool, Chris and Vicky were up in their room with their two dogs. Chris became agitated because Vicky spent money on the hotel room. Kenny told us that Chris yelled at Vicky the entire car ride to the hotel.

Jimmy decided to check on them. He could hear Chris yelling from the hallway. Once Vicky opened the door and let him in, Chris paced and stomped on the floor like he was marching, making himself angrier.

"Chris, do you want to go swimming?" Jimmy asked.

"No, I don't. I don't even want to be here," Chris replied.

"Oh, come on now, we can go swimming and get something to eat later on," Jimmy said, trying to defuse the situation.

"I don't want to be here and want to go home."

"Vicky, maybe he could go home, and you could stay?" Jimmy asked, trying to find a happy medium.

Chris ripped open a bag full of peanuts with his teeth, tilted his head back, opened his mouth, and let the peanuts fall in and to the side of his mouth.

"Fuck you. If I am going home, she is going home," Chris said as he charged toward Jimmy and pushed him. Jimmy fell back on the mirror and cracked the side of it. Chris swung his closed fist at Jimmy's face but missed.

Kenny had also come upstairs and quickly got between Jimmy and Chris. Vicky stayed in the room and argued with Chris. Vicky left a short time later with Chris and the dogs. Kenny stayed with us the entire weekend.

Their life wasn't the kind of life I wanted—addicted to drugs and without the ability to access proper mental health care, nor the

137

opportunity to escape the cycle of despair. The drug use escalated, and the fighting increased. But everything changed for the worse on May 14, 2012, when Vicky had a stroke caused by high blood pressure. The doctors said she died while on the Flight for Life ride from Puxico to Barnes Hospital in St. Louis. Her diagnosis was ultimately bleeding on the brain caused by Posterior Reversible Encephalopathy Syndrome (PRES). Vicky needed a stent implanted in an artery near her heart, and regular medication to control the hypertension and prevent another stroke from happening.

Vicky honestly believes she had a near-death experience where she went to heaven and was mistakenly sent back. When she was released from the hospital weeks later, she lost interest in the things she cared about, like her dogs and being a part of the community. She totally ignored her personal hygiene. She wasn't doing any housekeeping and had begun hoarding.

Before the stroke in 2012, she used to manage bills and the day-to-day upkeep of the trailer. After the stroke, she stayed home, reading the Bible and talking about heaven. Chris couldn't handle the responsibility of housekeeping or paying bills. He responded to the additional burden of caring for Vicky by taking more pills. He also stopped showering for weeks at a time. He would be in such a drug stupor that he smeared fecal matter on the walls of their bathroom.

Vicky was working to recover from the stroke but didn't feel like she was fully better. Anyone who has experienced a major health event like this needs months of rehabilitation. Sometimes the brain doesn't fully heal and cognitive functioning declines. Physically, she was still fragile. She told me that she started sleeping on the couch and stopped having sex with Chris. Her lack of interest in sex infuriated him. He told her that if she won't have sex with him, he would find someone else who will.

Chris had a lot of messed-up sexual issues. He raped his former sister-in-law from his first marriage. He pled to a lesser charge and should've been on a registered sex offender listing. I don't know what prompted it, but that September, Chris called me and wanted to apologize. He said that he had been sexually abused by his brother

138

and was raped by his sister. He explained that after his mother abandoned the family, he was molested and abused by his older siblings most of his life. He began to question his sexuality. Vicky was sickened by this information because she loved his family. We were confused why he was telling us these things, but after seeing his notebooks that we found in the trunk of Vicky's car it seems clear that Chris was struggling with some demons.

About a month after that phone call, which would have been in October 2012, Vicky called me wanting a blood transfusion because she thinks she has HIV/AIDS. I asked why she believes she has HIV. Vicky explained that during an argument with Chris, he admitted to having an ongoing threesome with his brother and his wife. Chris also told her he may have fathered his brother's child. She didn't understand what it meant that Chris had slept with a man; to her, men who slept with men got HIV/AIDS.

I asked to speak with Chris. He told me that the boy was his son and not his nephew and that it was common knowledge to his family. He didn't get a DNA test because that would mean ending the boy's Social Security and welfare benefits.

Vicky felt betrayed by Chris and his family. She took more drugs and became less connected to reality. She began to believe Chris was possessed by the devil. She refused to leave the house because she felt that the entire town of Puxico knew of the convoluted and possibly incestuous relationships in the Isaac family, and that everyone was laughing at her.

It wasn't just Chris and Vicky abusing opiates throughout the winter of 2012/2013. Chris, his brother Bobby, and his brother-in-law Cletus started going to more and new doctors to obtain hydrocodone. They also started selling Vicky's prescriptions. During one phone call, I asked Chris why he was doing this, and he said, "Social Security ain't paying [him] enough." I encouraged Vicky to get law enforcement involved for her own protection. She wouldn't. She said that she'd been to jail and didn't think Chris could handle it.

Even Chris' neighbors weren't immune to his actions. Vicky told me that once Chris went to a neighbor's house for a visit.

139

He asked to use the restroom, and while there, he went through the medicine cabinet and stole their prescription pills. After the neighbor realized his prescriptions disappeared, he confronted Chris and demanded the return of his drugs. Chris yelled and grabbed him by the shirt, tearing it open and popping all the buttons off. Vicky stopped the fight. She gave the man back his pills and begged him not to press charges. The man left, but Chris punched Vicky in the face and made her go to the doctor the next day to get new pills to make up for the stolen ones she returned.

The situation only got worse around Christmas when Kenny moved in. Vicky started calling me every few days, saying that she saw angels and that our dead mother was sitting on the bed speaking to her. And birds were telling her "the truth," but she wouldn't elaborate on what that "truth" was. I kept telling her she needed to get some help. I even called her primary physician, Dr. Kim, who agreed Vicky needed psychiatric help.

Kenny's presence contributed more stress to the household. Kenny had more of a contentious sibling relationship with her. You can't start being a mother to a 30-year-old man. In January 2013, a month after he moved in, Vicky and Kenny got into a physical altercation. Vicky believed Kenny was also laughing at her because of Chris' sexual relationship with his sister-in-law. Vicky called the Puxico Police Department and reported that Kenny acted like he was going to hug her but then began choking her. The police took a report, but they allowed Kenny to stay in the home.

Kenny was violent with Vicky. Chris was violent with Vicky too. On February 22, 2013, Vicky called and told me Chris punched her in the face because she wouldn't give him her pills. I asked Vicky to put Chris on the phone. When I asked Chris why he hit her, he said she needed to give him the pills because he was in pain. Chris said his old wrestling injury—an ankle—was hurting. I was scared for Vicky and called the Missouri Department of Health and Social Services hotline. A caseworker contacted me, and I told her the story. The caseworker and Puxico Marshal

140

Clark went to check on Vicky's well-being. Vicky told me later she was afraid to tell the caseworker the truth because everyone knew Chris' family, and Vicky believed they too were laughing at her for being a fool.

Chris took her phone away from her so she couldn't call me for the next two days. On my birthday, February 24th, Chris called me and said he was allowing Vicky to wish me a happy birthday. He handed the phone to her. Vicky said, "Chris won't let me have my medicine unless I stop making trouble for him." Chris took the phone back and asked me, "You don't want me to take her phone away from her again, do you?" He then hung up on me. That night I tried to get my sister Trixie to help me get legal guardianship of Vicky. She told me to mind my own business and that it was "just Chris being Chris."

She was one of the millions of people that accept and condone men having physical control of their partner. In rural areas of the country without adequate social services or private nonprofit groups to assist women experiencing spousal abuse, many are left to suffer until an inevitable and tragic outcome, resulting often in death, occurs.

Social service agencies were aware of Vicky's situation from both my calls and from incidents that occurred during another hospitalization. A few weeks after the birthday call, in March Vicky was taken from the trailer by ambulance to Poplar Bluff Regional Medical Center overnight for observation after she called 911 to report that she wasn't feeling right. She was released early the next morning, but Chris refused to pick her up. Vicky and I repeatedly called Chris for two and a half hours, but he would not drive the 30 miles from home to pick her up. Meanwhile, I was in my house in St. Louis unable to actually do anything besides make calls, so I called the Puxico Police Department, spoke to Marshal Clark, and requested a wellness check.

Within minutes of Marshal Clark going to the house, he called me and yelled, "The bitch got up there on her own. Let her fuckin' ass find a ride back."

141

I asked him why he wouldn't get her, but he only said, "She took her pills with her and *better have some pills left on her,*" then he hung up. I called the hospital and spoke to a social worker. She called me back about an hour later, letting me know that Chris finally picked up Vicky—four hours later. Yet no one seemed concerned that they were sending her home with someone who had just threatened her.

I called the Puxico Police Department in the morning and requested a wellness check on Vicky, but there was no answer. I called the Stoddard County Sheriff's Department to make the request, and a short time later Puxico City Marshal Clark called me. He said he knew Vicky was okay but didn't say if he actually went to the trailer to check on her. When I asked him about it, he hung up on me.

Vicky called me later that day and said she could only talk because Chris had left the trailer with his brother Eustice. Chris said he was afraid that with me involved, I would find out about their 'Medicaid scam' where they used each other's Medicaid cards to go to multiple doctors and get pills to sell.

Vicky already had a caseworker from Division of Aging who was supposed to be managing her case since her stroke. I called the caseworker to tell her about the hospital incident and asked about housing options in the area, in the hope that with an option of a different place to live, she could leave Chris.

Sometime in the middle of April, Vicky called me begging for help. She said, "Today is the day I am going to die. Chris and Eustice are coming back to get me." I heard a struggle, and the phone landed on the floor. Through the phone, I could hear Chris tell Vicky, "Eustice and I have hired Omar—to kill you if you don't give us those pills. He has diplomatic immunity, and they will never convict him." I hung up the phone and called Puxico Police, and once again Marshal Clark told me, "He is just talking talk." I then called the Division of Aging caseworker to report this, and she told me to call the police. I told her I already did. She said she could not do any more for me. I again called my sister in Georgia and asked for help to obtain guardianship, and she told her to mind my own business.

I kept calling Vicky's phone, and about an hour later, Chris answered. I calmly asked him if Vicky could come up to St. Louis for a visit. I had to try to get her out of that house.

He said, "Fuck you. She has to go to the doctor because she owes me pills," and hung up. I called the Drug Enforcement Agency (DEA) and spoke to a special agent who said to contact the physician prescribing the pills. The DEA agent said these types of cases were hard to prove because you have to be at the appointments when the people are using fraudulent cards. I called the Pain Center, where they got the pills from, and told the physician's assistant about the alleged scheme, and he promised to keep an eye out for any discrepancies.

Everything settled down for about a week, and then I received another call from Vicky saying she was afraid she was going to die because Chris was now taking her seizure medicine. She finally wanted to find out about divorce. I called the Legal Aid office on my other line and conferenced Vicky in. I had the divorce proceeding paperwork sent to her house. I was tired of these calls, but I called an attorney in Stoddard County to ask about starting the paperwork for legal guardianship of Vicky. I told him I would be in the area soon to file the paperwork.

My next call was to her primary physician, and I informed him that I was working on getting legal guardianship. He told me that he had referred her for psychiatric assistance for some time. Later that same day Vicky called, and I could hear Chris yelling in the background. I asked to speak with him. I asked what he was mad about. He said, "She took all the pills." I tried to calm him down and then asked if I could have guardianship of her. He got mad and said, "Fuck you. She is staying right here. I need her Social Security to pay bills." He hung up on me.

Five days before the murder, Kenny called 911 saying he was going to kill Vicky and Chris and then himself. Kenny said he was tired of the constant fighting and pill usage. The Puxico Police arrived, and Kenny was placed in the psychiatric ward at the Poplar Bluff Regional Medical Center for observation.

Vicky's mental state continued to decline. She texted me to say our mom came to her and that Mom told her that our older sister stole Mom's ring off her finger at the funeral home before she was buried. Vicky believed that our sister and brother are also possessed by the devil.

A couple days later, Kenny was released from the hospital. The day I got the divorce paperwork from Legal Aid, Vicky said she and Chris were now getting along well, and she felt sorry for him because he was molested by his brothers and sisters. The day before the murder, Chris and Vicky took out a $1,500 loan from the Bank of Advance. Chris spent a couple of hundred dollars on his brother's children—including the boy Chris believed was his son—buying them all new shoes.

The next call from Puxico came from Kenny telling me that Chris was dead and Vicky was in jail.

Patti Tucka heard all this with a quiet and reserved silence. I couldn't tell if she was stunned or was that skilled in concealing her emotions. After a short pause she said, "Well, that's a lot to take in."

Ms. Tucka had listened closely and researched the details I told her. She gave me her thoughts on how she was going to proceed with the trial and more information about Chris' history of violence. He had been married before and it was during that period he was accused of rape.

"Chris' ex-wife had contacted law enforcement during their marriage. The ex-wife said she was married to Chris from 1992 to April 1995. She said he physically abused her on multiple occasions, but she only reported him to the police once. When she tried to leave Chris, he threw a knife and almost hit her face. Her family member was the victim in the rape case Chris pleaded guilty to," she told me.

"Is she going to be subpoenaed?" I asked.

"Yes, if and when we go to trial," she said with a sigh.

"What do you mean? Has a plea deal been offered?"

"No, but things can change once we get closer to the trial date."

CHAPTER NINE

*V*icky called to tell us she saw Kenny at his taped deposition as she was legally allowed to be present with her attorney, Ms. Tucka. She thought he looked thin and tired. He spoke in that same fake accent throughout his entire statement. Although he hadn't seen Vicky in over a year, he wouldn't look her or anyone else in the eyes. Kenny's appearance shook Vicky.

"I am tired of them going after Kenny. Just let me rot in jail but leave him alone. Like Mom said, I made my bed, I have to lie in it," she told me during our weekend phone call.

"The best thing you can do is work on getting out of jail and taking care of Kenny," I told her.

Two days later, Vicky, against my advice, decided to accept a plea deal of guilty to second-degree murder. The state had initially charged her with first-degree murder and armed criminal action. Ms. Tucka told her the judge, and not a jury, would now decide her actual sentence, but she didn't expect Vicky to get sentenced to more than 25 years. I wasn't so sure or so confident as Ms. Tucka. Vicky had just pled guilty to killing her husband, a man with longstanding familial relationships in Stoddard County. We already experienced three years of "rural justice" in Stoddard County, and I had a feeling that the County wasn't done with her yet.

I flew into St. Louis from Seattle on December 14th for the sentencing hearing. The day was also Kenny's birthday and the day before Mom's birthday. She would have been 84 years old. I drove the three hours south to Poplar Bluff with the intention of picking up Kenny. He had seemed to be doing better since being released from his six-month incarceration in the Stoddard County Jail. I bought him a new cell phone and he had been calling us regularly to check in. Yet when I tried to call Kenny when we landed, the call went directly to voicemail.

We had made a plan that Kenny would meet us in Poplar Bluff and we would attend Vicky's sentencing hearing. Then he would return to Seattle with us. We would start the conservatorship process all over again and give him access to quality mental health care. I should have started worrying that evening when he didn't show up that evening to meet us at the hotel as we had planned.

The next morning, I drove 45 miles to Kennett, Missouri, to find out Vicky's fate. I had hoped that Kenny would be at the hotel in Poplar Bluff when I returned. I convinced myself that he couldn't watch Vicky get sentenced for the crime he committed.

As this was a sentencing trial, I could speak on Vicky's behalf in a plea for mercy. I was the only one in the courtroom to support Vicky. The Isaac family was represented by Chris' father, Donald, and his seven siblings.

I pulled up to the Dunklin County Justice Center. A female deputy assisted me through the metal detector. I asked her about the location of the sentencing hearing. As I went around the corner, I saw Eustice, Doris, and other members of the extended Isaac family. I heard a woman's voice over the crowd noise say, "There's Vicky's sister. Look at that bitch." Then I saw Eustice say under his breath but loud enough to hear, "I need to put my dick in her ass." It was a revelation of his true self and not the kindly, churchgoing façade he presented to the world.

When I walked into the courtroom, Elmer Isaac stood alone in the first row. There were two court staffers in the room as well. The courtroom looked like the dozens of courtrooms I had been in testifying for the prosecution, with a judge's chair behind an elevated bench and on either side, the American flag and the State of Missouri flag. The state seal hung on the wall above the judge's chair, standing out in bright contrast to the dark wood paneling covering the walls and jury box. But this was not a typical recitation of objective facts style of testimony. I needed to convey the truth of my sister's suffering—not just during her marriage to Chris, but throughout her entire life—to the judge. I was the only one who could and would bear witness to the abuse, trauma, and struggles she faced. I was testifying for my sister's life.

I was alone in the courtroom and beginning to worry after hearing the Isaacs' threats and vulgar remarks, and decided to

146

stay near a deputy. As I again walked past the family, Eustice said, "That's the one that needs a bullet, not my brother."

I found a female deputy and asked if I could stand next to her, and let her know what the Isaac family had been saying to me. A few of Vicky's old friends from Poplar Bluff sat in the back of the courtroom. I sat in the front row behind Patti Tucka. Vicky was led into the courtroom wearing an orange jumpsuit with her hands chained in front of her. She smiled as she saw us and took her seat.

The Stoddard County prosecutor, Russ Oliver, stood on the prosecution side of the courtroom with the Isaac family. He was one of the "hometown boys done good." Born and raised in Stoddard County, his suit would have been considered modest in St. Louis but was fancy for Stoddard County. He and I might have had a good working relationship as a Prosecutor and Police Chief in another place and time, but now he looked at me like I was the same kind of trash he judged Vicky to be. But, then again, from how he chose to pursue this case, he wouldn't care for my modern approach to police work based on scientific evidence and compassionate service to citizens. He never once looked at me, Ms. Tucka, or Vicky, and stood there laughing and talking to the Isaac family.

The prosecutor called each and every member of the Isaac family one by one to the stand. We were told by Vicky's lawyer, Ms. Tucka, that there would be no cross-examination or rebuttal to anything the witnesses said. The family blamed all of Vicky and Chris' problems on her.

Doris claimed that Vicky bragged she "didn't care if she went to jail because it would be a vacation." Another sister, Angelica Settles, a State of Missouri licensed social worker, turned to the judge and said, "Judge Mayer, you have known me and my family for a long time." At that exact moment, I knew Vicky was doomed to spend the rest of her natural life in prison. No more Thanksgiving dinners, flea market shopping, or visiting with the neighbors. I heard the song "The Night the Lights Went Out in Georgia" echoing in my head, "*Don't trust your soul to no backwoods*

Southern lawyer. 'Cause the judge in the town's got bloodstains on his hands."

Then it was Ms. Tucka's turn to make her argument for compassion for Vicky. I was the first to be called. She had me state my name and occupation. I looked up and faced the gallery as I was speaking and saw Eustice mouth the word "whore" at me. I held my head high and continued with my testimony. I gave a short yet impassioned history of Vicky's struggles and explained how Vicky was a victim of childhood and spousal abuse.

The prosecutor addressed the judge and gallery and said, "Let's get this straight. There is only one victim here." He glared at me. I stared straight back at him.

Judge Mayer read his sentence. It didn't matter what he actually said. I was so upset because I knew this case had been decided a long time ago. What we were sitting through, what the citizens and we were paying for, was a farce. Vicky didn't have a chance at fairness or rehabilitation. Chris' life had been brutally ended in this endless cycle of abuse, and yet no one actually helped Chris, Vicky, or even Kenny before events took this fatally tragic turn.

Everyone stood up for the judge to leave. Vicky expected the judge to hand down a sentence of 25 years, like Ms. Tucka worked with the prosecutor's office to arrange in the plea deal. The reality of the life sentence sank in and Vicky began yelling obscenities in a fit of hopeless rage. Three deputies tackled and restrained her. The prosecutor smiled and looked at me as a male deputy beat Vicky across the back with a metal baton. I looked at him and said, "We'll appeal this."

The Isaac family approached me. Angelica stood in my face and said, "Your sister ain't nothing but a murderer."

The temper I had kept under control for so long finally snapped, I answered her right back, "Your brother wasn't nothing but a child rapist. He pled guilty to sexual assault," I said. The entire family of dozens of people began to surround me as I quickly found the exit to make my way to safety from the volatile Isaac family.

I drove out of the parking lot. I needed to find Kenny in Poplar Bluff before he heard the news of Vicky's life sentence to prison on the television. I drove around for hours looking for Kenny as I called his phone. Nothing. No answer. The calls clicked over to voicemail and there was no sign of Kenny near his usual haunts. Exhausted and defeated, I gave up and headed to my hotel room.

I sat on the bed trying to recover from the shock of the sentence while my phone was pinging and buzzing with social media notifications. I didn't want to look or reply but relented when the noise wouldn't stop. It wasn't Kenny calling, it was my friends asking if I had been arrested. I had no idea where they got that idea. But I soon found out.

The Stoddard County prosecutor took it upon himself to write a press release for the local KFVS television news station which read in part:

> *According to Stoddard County Prosecuting Attorney Russell Oliver, right after the hearing, Isaac and her sister, Betty Frizzell, started screaming obscenities and threatened physical violence toward the victim's family along with others in the court.*
>
> *There was an apparent struggle in the courtroom, and Isaac was restrained by court bailiffs. But, her sister, Betty Frizzell, ran from the courthouse and hasn't been seen since.*
>
> *Witnesses filled out statements about the incident in the courtroom and have been submitted to the Dunklin County Prosecuting Attorney.*
>
> *Frizzell may face charges in connection to the incident.*[1]

The Daily American Republic, the Poplar Bluff newspaper, put Vicky's case on the front page, including the lies about me attacking people and running off. The newspaper took their story directly from the prosecutor—they didn't contact me for a statement. The newspaper I learned to read from as a child turned on me.

---

1 https://www.kfvs12.com/story/34067102/puxico-woman-sentenced-to-prison-for-murder-of-her-husband/

I have dedicated my adult life to upholding the law. I even received the State of Missouri award for Law Enforcement Officer of the Year. But living for the past few years in a progressive city in a West Coast state, I forgot that a woman, even a former Chief of Police, is to be seen and not heard in southeast Missouri. In the eyes of the judge, the prosecutor, and all those good-old-boys in every jailhouse and courthouse in these backward bootheel counties, I was nothing more than a little girl. Same as if I was back in my second grade class being called white trash, but this time I'm not holding a crayon; I've earned two master's degrees and logged years of experience in criminal justice. They made the mistake of underestimating me.

CHAPTER TEN

On December 19, 2016, Vicky was transported to Women's Eastern Reception, Diagnostic and Correctional Center, located almost two hours northwest of St. Louis and one of the two women's prisons in Missouri. Once she arrived, her property was inventoried. After inventory, she took a shower and went through the booking process of being photographed and fingerprinted again and issued an identification number. For the rest of her natural life the State of Missouri refers to Vicky as inmate number 80172.

Vicky would be placed in a permanent facility after mental and medical assessments were completed. I knew I wouldn't be allowed to visit her for the first two weeks after she arrived, but I had already sent in my application to the Department of Corrections, who would conduct a criminal background check to determine whether or not I *could* visit her.

I tried to hide my worry about Kenny from Vicky in our weekly calls. She adjusted well to life in prison. She hadn't used opiates since her arrest, so gone were the hallucinations the drugs created in her fragile mind. The dietary restrictions and a food schedule imposed by the prison helped her to lose weight for the first time in years. The hardest adjustment to prison was living around so many people. Vicky didn't like having five roommates and wanted to transfer to the smaller Chillicothe Correctional Center, about two hours east of Kansas City, Missouri. Chillicothe had an active Christian program and a Puppies for Parole (PFP) program that works with inmates to train and socialize shelter dogs. A program like the PFP would be good for Vicky's mental health.

But I couldn't sleep. I kept thinking about Kenny. Hurt and alone somewhere. I trusted my instincts—they've kept me alive while patrolling dangerous places—and those instincts told me that something was wrong with Kenny. Mom used to say, "Betty is smart because she knows things we don't or can't know. She was born with a veil on her face." It was an old wives' tale that when a baby was born with the amniotic sac intact, it was called "a veil" and conveyed extrasensory powers. I wished I had some mystical wisdom to tell me where Kenny was.

I woke with my nightmares that someone from the Isaac family killed Kenny. I had found out that it was Chris' nephew Gabriel who beat Kenny last year. I didn't trust him or his mother, Crystal. She was the sister who Chris claimed raped him as a child. Gabriel had a lengthy criminal history, and at the time Kenny was assaulted, was on unsupervised probation for four years for a guilty plea on a second-degree assault charge.

I made a deal with myself: if Kenny missed his scheduled trial date on January 18, 2017, I would file a missing person report. He never showed up. On January 24, 2017, I filed a report with the Monroe, Washington Police Department. In the description, I listed Kenny as 6'6" tall, 180 pounds, blond hair and blue eyes, with a large tattoo of the word "Firewood" across his neck. As I wrote the word "Firewood" on the page, I would've given anything to hear Kenny say, "Oh, Firewood is okay." He may have seemed big and tough, but he was still making his "bird calls" and was a little lost pigeon in a rough, unforgiving world.

The items Kenny left in the hotel upon his release from Stoddard County Jail in early December finally arrived at home in Washington state. The package contained one shirt, a couple pairs of pants, and a large bound scrapbook. I flipped through the book and realized it was a copy of his entire personal history compiled for his Social Security application. Nearly three thousand pages of medical and educational records and notes regarding his condition. It was the first time I had ever seen what professionals had to say about Kenny. And what Kenny had to say about himself.

He reported "homicidal ideation" about six months before the murder, according to one doctor. He told another doctor that he left his job at the riverboat barge company because he was afraid he would hurt someone. He even told the doctors that he was Catholic though he had never set foot in a Catholic church in his life. Then there were his own rantings: that he'd been drugged and shot many times, that the police were after him and would brag on television about killing him. His paranoia was uncontrolled.

The forms we tried to get him to sign for conservatorship were purposefully avoided. He didn't want it. He didn't want me to speak to his doctors and didn't want them to release any information to me. He told them that I had an "agenda." Reading through the book made it more explicit that Kenny, in the grips of his mental illness, and not Vicky, shot Chris that May morning.

I had more than enough reasons than ever to get a complete copy of those police and forensic reports. It took years of filing "Sunshine Law" requests but now that Vicky's trial and sentencing were over, I could at least get a copy of her case file from her attorney, and review what the police and prosecutors had done to my family over the past three and a half years.

Odd things popped up in the files. I discovered that only Kenny—not Vicky—was tested for gunshot residue. But the deputies only tested his right hand, not his left hand, which is his shooting hand. They didn't take his clothing, and they didn't take a DNA swab to test against the gun.

The initial 911 call also piqued my interest. According to the report, Vicky called 911 to say she shot her husband. After Vicky confessed, Kenny took over the phone conversation. He answered all the questions and did all the talking. The first officer on the scene reported:

"I received a call from Stoddard County that a woman had called from 365 Church Street reporting that she shot her husband. The call was about 8:18 a.m. and I arrived at 8:28 a.m. I observed the resident, Vicky Isaac, sitting on the porch with blood on her hands. I asked her what happened and she didn't reply but her son Kenny who standing on the porch said they weren't arguing. He walked into the hallway to get him something to drink at five. I didn't ask questions but Kenneth kept talking saying that he heard what he thought was gunshots and wanted to see it and saw his mother Vicky standing over the victim. She was pointing a gun at Chris's head and fired three or four more rounds. I asked where the gun was now. Kenneth said it was laying on the floor at this time."[1]

---

1 Report from police

The most disappointing thing I learned was that the first officer who interviewed Kenny at Puxico Police Department didn't record the interview. The officer, a Chief Deputy, said in a deposition that Puxico didn't have a tape recorder available. The ability to record an interview provides security for the officer and the people being interviewed. It is ludicrous to think in the year 2013 that a police department wouldn't have a functioning audio recording device and interview protocol in place.

I didn't understand until I looked at their Uniformed Crime Reporting (UCR) on the Missouri State Highway Patrol Statistical Analysis Website. In 2013, the year Vicky was arrested, the Puxico Police Department reported one criminal homicide, no rapes, no attempted rapes, no robberies, no aggravated assaults, no burglaries, one larceny-theft, two vehicle thefts, no arson, one violent crime, and three property crimes for a grand total of seven arrests. Yet, the taxpayers paid for a Police Chief and four officers.

I have, and other law enforcement professionals and academics have, a theory about rural policing: towns with a population under 2,500 don't need an independent police department and are better served by either a robust and expanded county Sheriff's Department or a unified policing district.

Small departments are fundamentally at a disadvantage. They have limited funds to acquire suitable candidates for positions and are often left with a hiring pool of what a Saint Louis University study dubbed "*Muni shufflers*": officers who get in trouble and resign before they're fired, then move to a new department bringing their bad habits with them. Or they hire inexperienced officers starting out their careers, and small towns chew rookie officers up and spit them out by overworking them and not providing them with the proper field training officer. The small-town law enforcement environment doesn't foster skills like report writing, legal interviewing, and evidence handling skills to make concrete cases. The end result is trust issues between the community and its police department, leaving citizens feeling targeted and unsafe in their homes.

In the case file, I found another deposition from the second officer who interviewed Kenny an hour after the first interview. This time it was recorded. The officer described Kenny as *"little upset obviously he carried on a conversation with us at times. I don't remember him crying or anything. He may have. I don't remember but I could tell you he was concerned about what happened what he just witnessed. He talked about the events of that morning."*

This was hardly the testimony of a highly trained officer. After four years of protecting Vicky's feelings, I needed to know the truth for myself. I needed to talk to her.

𝕴n July, Julian and I flew to Missouri for a visit with old friends in St. Louis, and then drove to Chillicothe to visit Vicky at her new prison location. Chillicothe is a small town with a population of about 9,000, mostly white residents. The prison is the city's focal point, as its large parking lot is visible from Highway 65. Visitors walk up to a large tin-roofed concrete building with a simple handmade "Visiting" sign hanging over the door, making it look more like a rest stop than a prison.

The line was long and filled with older men waiting to see women they had met online. For some, it was the first visit as they brought homemade food to share with their pen pals, and for others, it was an ongoing relationship that brought companionship to their lonely lives.

Vicky had asked Julian and me to wear rock band T-shirts and give her a bit of rock 'n' roll. A female guard told me that I wouldn't be allowed in because my jeans had shredded knees. Luckily, I had our luggage in the car. I was allowed to change clothes and come back as Julian held my place in the line. I just wanted to see Vicky. We made our way up to a glass window, and the corrections officer checked our names and took our identification. Then we were led into a room, through a metal detector, and then to a smaller room painted with cheery cartoon figures meant to bring a sense of normalcy for children visiting their mothers. Vending machines filled with candy and snacks lined the right wall.

155

We waited at the door until Vicky emerged from the locked doors. She was smiling and looked prettier than I had seen her in years. It's awful to think about how bad her life was out in the so-called free world that going to prison gave her a path to so much happiness. For the first time since 2013, I got to hug my sister. She was giggly and happy. We talked about our trip and took pictures.

Julian knew I wanted to talk to Vicky privately and, after some small talk, took himself for a leisurely visit to the vending machines. I didn't have much time to beat around the bush; I needed straight answers.

"All right, Vicky, there's nobody here but us. I need to know. Did you really do this? Did you shoot Chris?" I asked.

"Yeah, yeah. I did it. I was me," she said as she looked down at her feet.

"Are you sure Kenny didn't do this?" I sternly asked her.

"No, it was me." She answered without looking me in the eye. I had seen this maneuver a million times. It was Vicky's tell, her unconscious giveaway that she was lying. She did it whenever Mom asked her something that she didn't want to answer truthfully. Whatever words she said, the downward gaze at her shoes told me the truth. At that moment, I knew in my heart she didn't kill Chris. She did not commit the crime she was convicted of. I was angry all over again. Vicky thinks she is doing the right thing for her son, and Kenny shows how much he loved her by running off. One thing we country women are good at is punishing ourselves for the failings of our family.

All too soon, our visiting time was over, and we said our goodbyes. I heard Vicky say in her little girl voice, "I wish I was coming home with you." It reminded me of us as children blowing all the seeds off a dandelion with a single breath. The despair in her voice was heart-wrenching. Julian started to cry. I fought back those tears, knowing that my tears wouldn't save her and that one day I would be back at that prison to bring her home with us.

156

CHAPTER ELEVEN

I had spent so much time during the past four years taking care of everyone else I had lost myself. I decided to go visit Mom's grave in the family graveyard; I needed to tell her a few things. I also needed to put everything I knew about her and our lives into its proper place. Her overwhelming presence in life had become a specter of remembered pain. Could I find and separate the terrible things she did to Vicky and me from the good? I wanted to believe that Mom did better by us than her mother Roxie did by her. And I know I was a loving and supportive mother to my son. Could I finally break the cycle of abuse?

The cemetery was in a hidden section at the end of a forgotten gravel country road off Highway NN. The pine trees were tall, and plenty stood like welcoming family relatives. The sun would beam through those trees like a spotlight shining down on the graves of the long gone. There was not even a sign which told the name of the graveyard. The cemetery was surrounded by a cheap wire fence, with two old-fashioned arch-shaped gates. The Frizzell family had relatives buried there since the early 1900s. It was littered with a mix of tombstones, from simple homemade ones made of wood and every other material you could imagine, to precisely carved limestone. Mom loved to tell us about each person that lay in those graves.

I had helped Mom clean the family graveyard when I was young. Like most children, I didn't understand the significance of knowing one's past. I would rather be home riding a bicycle or listening to music than out digging in the dirt. Each year with the change of the seasons, Mom, Vicky, and I would pack up the car and head to the country. We would mow the grass, clean the leaves off the graves, and pick up whatever trash was flying around. It was hours of hard manual labor, but it also meant peaceful time with Mom. At home, we were always careful as every interaction was colored by our fear of her mighty temper. Mom was different in this country graveyard. We all felt the presence of our history, our people. It was not sad, but it was a somber and reverent occasion, this task for caring for our family history. Her worn, scarred, and work-battered hands showed the respect she had for the place and those buried there. Her right hand bore a large scar from a chainsaw, gotten from clearing trees years ago, yet she continued to clean the gravesites every year until she died. Cleaning the graveyard was a tribute to her beloved yet flawed daddy, and a way to be close to him. She remembered the fights and the drinking, but she found a way to love him anyway.

It wasn't until I was older and moved away from this place that I learned to appreciate the family graveyard. It and Mom were links to a past that was painful and yet had glimmers of happiness. I needed to find the good and find my strength. Now, underneath Mom's favorite pine tree, I stood at her leaf-covered grave, eyes full of tears, praying for the energy to keep fighting for Vicky and Kenny. Mom never showed weakness even if she felt it.

Our last conversation on the night before her death was the best we ever had. As we got ready for bed, Mom wanted to talk. Julian and Kenny were playing a game in the bedroom while Mom and I sat in the front room watching the news.

"Betty," Mom said, breaking the silence. "There are things I'll take to my grave with me. I have done bad things and good things that no one will ever know about," she solemnly told me.

"What things?" I asked, knowing I wouldn't get a straight answer.

"Things... and a lot of regrets," she replied, straightening out her white flannel nightgown.

"What kind of regrets?" I asked again, knowing there would never be any resolution to my question.

"Lots. But I want you to know I am proud of you. You did something with your life. The rest of the kids did nothing, but you went out and made something of yourself," she said with tears in her eyes.

"I haven't done nothing." I swallowed my tears, determined not to cry.

"Well, I better get to bed." She sat the recliner up and walked to her room.

"I love you," she said.

"Love you too," I replied. This was one of the five times she ever told me she loved me.

Remembering this old story strengthened me. I came from a people that fought for what they loved. I didn't need to cry. I needed to pick myself back up and dig down deep into that well of whatever kept Mom going all those years. I needed to do what my family does best—fight. But first, I needed to fight for myself.

Women in my family don't live to see 75. Grandma Roxie died at age 72. Mom died at age 68. Diabetes and heart disease haunt each generation like a ghost from the previous one. Combine bad genes with a sugary carbohydrate diet shaped by poverty, and limited access to health care resulted in preventable illnesses growing into crises and sad endings to our lives. We love too hard, carry too many burdens, and die too soon.

I was quickly following my ancestors' steps by living the same unhealthy way and slowly killing myself. The constant stress of the past few years left me a shell of the confident woman I fought so hard to become. All the degrees and awards in the world didn't erase the deep self-loathing and hurt. And then I would think about how I failed Vicky and Kenny. I knew what happens to people like Vicky in prison. They are often revictimized by unethical guards and other inmates. Her inability to control her behavior would result in punishment, which in prison meant revoking privileges and, in the worst case, numerous days in solitary confinement. Thinking about her fate made me a nervous wreck. Thinking about Kenny made me sick to my stomach. Where was Kenny? Was he even alive?

I ate my pain and drowned my hurt in food. Eating was a quick fix to forget about the horrors Vicky could face and Kenny's disappearance. I ballooned up to 335 pounds. My diabetes was barely controlled. I was on the fast track to dying like all the women in my family. I had a reckoning with myself: I did not want to die young. I wanted to live. I was born to be a grandmother, but if I didn't get my food issues and health under control, I would never see Julian meet someone to love and start a family with. His children wouldn't know their grandmother. I needed help.

I talked to my doctor during a check-up and she suggested I consider gastric bypass surgery. To qualify for gastric bypass surgery, I was required to seek mental health counseling—something unheard of in my family. Mom refused to talk to anyone about her inner struggles. She always said, "Keep that stuff to yourself. Then people can't use it against you." I decided that I couldn't get my eating under control by myself, and to not let stubbornness and shame prevent me from getting the help I needed.

I was reluctant to begin therapy, as much as I intellectually knew it could help me. Mom had warned us repeatedly about telling family secrets and how "people wouldn't take you seriously because they will think you're crazy," but I wanted to free myself from this cycle of self-abuse. I wasn't alone in turning to food as a way to hide my feelings. According to a study of people who receive bariatric surgery, a sizable majority of medically obese patients were found to have endured childhood trauma. The study also found that people who were maltreated during childhood experienced a more significant number of mental health diagnoses over their lifetime than people who did not experience abuse. Physical and emotional neglect, emotional or sexual abuse directly lead to higher numbers of mood and anxiety disorder diagnoses.

My therapist diagnosed me with post-traumatic stress disorder, anxiety, depression, and obsessive-compulsive disorder. For the first time in my life, I had names for the feelings inside of me. When you're going through trauma, you don't see it as trauma—it's just living life. I began to wonder if Mom had had access to better health care, she could have understood exactly how much trauma her violent and turbulent childhood caused in her life.

I slowly realized the life I was living was not the life I wanted. My husband Jimmy and I had grown apart. Yes, there were good years, but I held him back from true happiness because I didn't love him in the way he deserved. My husband, like Kenny, is learning-disabled and has issues affecting his short-term memory.

160

Unlike Kenny, who was encouraged to embrace his disability, Jimmy's parents shamed him into thinking his learning disability was an embarrassment. Our relationship was unequal—more like a mother and child. In my unhealthy worldview tainted by a repressive church teaching and burdened with moral scrupulosity, I could not allow myself the "failure" of divorce, even if it was the best solution for everyone. I'm pleased to say that with therapy—individual and family—Jimmy and I are happily divorced and remain excellent friends and committed parents.

My life was not the only one that began to change. Vicky continued to flourish in Chillicothe Penitentiary. Through the Christian program she found a prison ministry that supported her, and fell back in love with the church. She is not the first, nor will she be the last, to find solace in the Lord when at the lowest point of their life and in the scariest of places. For Vicky, being in the church group gave her a real community with people who accepted her as born again in the spirit and perfect in God's eyes. The prison also provided her regular healthcare that included mental health. She was taking her medicine regularly and speaking with a psychiatrist and was happier than I knew her to be in years.

While Vicky was adjusting to life in prison and I was on my own path of recovery, Kenny's disappearance was still a source of stress and an open legal matter. Two months after filing Kenny's missing person report, I received a call from a Detective Phelps with the Poplar Bluff Police Department. He informed me that he was the detective assigned to the case. I had never spoken to him before.

"Mr. Smith is your nephew, correct?" he asked.

"Yes, he is my sister's son."

"When is the last time you spoke with Mr. Smith?"

"In December 2016, right before my sister's sentencing trial. He had been in Stoddard County Jail on a theft charge for six months and was released in early December. Kenny was supposed to meet us in Poplar Bluff so he could come with us to see Vicky at the sentencing, and then we had arranged for him to come back to Seattle with us. He never showed up."

"That was the last time anyone heard from him?"

"Yes. Kenny has mental health issues and can't really take care of himself. We're worried because the family of the victim from my sister's case allegedly attacked Kenny when he was living by himself in downtown Poplar Bluff."

I could hear him writing the information down.

"How could he be supporting himself?"

"He has Social Security benefits."

Kenny in high school,
Poplar Bluff, Missouri 1997

"Ms. Frizzell, thank you for the information. I will be getting back to you."

The call seemed brief, and I think he thought this was going to be a quick case. He probably thought Kenny was in a psychiatric ward of the hospital, on the streets, or in jail.

After a few days, Detective Phelps called me.

"Ms. Frizzell, did you know Kenny had a passport?"

"No. How in the hell did he get a passport? He can barely read or write."

"He has a passport. I am checking with Homeland Security to see if he left the country. It may take a couple of days."

"Thank you. Anything you can do helps."

Kenny had trouble filling out job applications. It was hard to believe he went through the process of gathering the materials and filling out the application for a passport. Kenny was diagnosed as

162

learning-disabled; he had a fourth-grade reading level and an IQ of 64.

A few hours later, my worry was turned up to eleven when Detective Phelps called again. He told me that Kenny's bank account hadn't been accessed for months. He had thousands of dollars in his account from the monthly Social Security deposits, but the last transaction was months ago in Milan, Italy!

Was he dead and the card stolen? That was improbable because they would have cleared out his bank account. My mind was reeling with the possibilities. I thought, *there is no way he is in Italy.* I wanted to laugh, but in Kenny's flawed logic and mental state, now convinced he was Catholic, who knows what the truth was.

On March 27, 2017, I received another call from Detective Phelps, who told me the story as he understood it. On December 12, 2016, a person fitting Kenny's description presented his passport and boarded Air Berlin flight #7421 for Berlin, Germany. Once the flight landed, he purchased an additional ticket for Air Berlin flight #8704 from Berlin to Rome, Italy. That's all he knew and suggested I contact the State Department.

Due to the nine-hour time difference, I had to wait until early the next morning to speak to someone. I could barely sleep that night and woke up three hours later to call the Consulate in Rome. I told them the entire story and then emailed Kenny's pictures and all the documents relating to his troubles, Vicky's troubles, and our troublesome family relationships as proof that our shared blood and troubles bound us together.

The next morning, a Consulate representative called, ready to speak and fill in the details on Kenny's missing months. The Consulate, too, had been attempting to piece together the story of the man who arrived in Rome in December of 2016 and was admitted to hospital in early January of 2017. Kenny was in terrible physical shape and told the staff that he was looking for his twin sister because the rest of his family had been killed in a house fire. He'd been wearing the same socks and shoes for months, and his feet had become infected. The hospital notes that his socks were enmeshed with the flesh as the infection spread and became gangrenous. Surgeons amputated both of his feet and part of one leg to stop the spread of the toxins released by the infecting bacteria. He was given prosthetics and learned to walk with them but was not well enough to leave the hospital. But he was alive. Kenny was alive.

I explained Kenny's mental health issues again, and that none of what he told the Consulate staff or the hospital staff was true. The Consulate said Kenny would have to leave Italy as soon as possible because he had overstayed his visa. I would have to pay for the flight back to the U.S. if I couldn't access his benefits.

I walked into the Social Security office in Everett, Washington, and explained to the older woman, who had probably heard a lifetime of crazy stories in her job but never one as convoluted as this. She looked at me like I was the one who had issues and reached under her deck for the silent alarm. I said, "Oh, no. Wait. I have the paperwork. I have a police report, the email from the U.S. Consulate, and the phone number for Detective Phelps." She took my application for payee benefits and said it would take ten days for Kenny to appeal. Ten days was too long. I would have to pay for Kenny's plane ticket.

I received an email from the Consulate representative who spoke to Kenny's doctor. He would be discharged on May 3, 2017. It was not cheap to purchase a last-minute one-way ticket with handicap accessibility from Rome to Seattle, but I managed it.

The day before Kenny left Rome, the Consulate emailed to let me know that Kenny was doing well with his prosthetic feet, and he was able to walk with some assistance. On May 3, 2017, Kenny boarded the plane in Rome, Italy, and was supposed to arrive in Seattle at 9 p.m. on May 3rd. We took a car service to Sea-Tac airport outside of Seattle, ready to welcome the wayward traveler home. I had even purchased a used wheelchair. He never arrived.

I made phone calls and more phone calls. To airlines. To the State Department. To the Consulate in Rome. To the Consulate in Frankfurt, where his connecting flight from Rome landed and he was supposed to be escorted to the flight to Seattle. I filed a missing person report with the airport police at Sea-Tac, and they kindly began checking for Kenny at other nearby airports. No one would take responsibility for how Kenny went missing, but everyone assured me they were searching for him. Everyone was baffled how a profoundly disturbed, heavily tattooed, disheveled American amputee could have disembarked from an Italian airplane unseen and disappeared in Frankfurt, Germany like a wisp of steam.

I was furious. I don't know who I was angry at—Kenny, the airlines, the Consulate, Vicky, or myself. Maybe I was just mad at everyone.

In November of 2018, I got a solid lead from the German police about Kenny. It had been nearly an entire year since his disappearance. I'd been saving money and vacation days for the past year in the hope that this day would come. I had mixed feelings; I was convinced he killed Chris, and his mother was in prison for his crime, but he was still my nephew, my blood. He was a part of my family, and though his mental illness had robbed him of sanity, that illness didn't erase his right to proper health care, both psychological and physical. It didn't take away his family, who would continue to fight for him to get the help he needed.

Jimmy and Kenny had enjoyed a close relationship, and having Jimmy with me would help convince Kenny to come back to the States. We flew from Seattle to Frankfurt in early November. The last sighting of Kenny was around the Frankfurt Main train station, the Hauptbahnhof. We may have looked like American tourists as we rode the trains amongst people going about their daily lives, but we were looking for a schizophrenic man with no feet.

The station, just like the rest of Frankfurt, is a mixture of old and new. The architecture is a combination of Neo-Renaissance and neoclassical styles. The outside was built in the late 19th century, with later pieces added. Inside the station's platform hall, arch-shaped steel girders with windows allow the light to come through to the tiled floors. The restaurants reminded me of

165

the U.S.: Dunkin' Donuts, McDonald's, and downstairs a Burger King. There were hundreds of dark gray pigeons everywhere. The pigeons didn't care about the thousands of passengers moving back and forth. This was their house. The people were part of their world. The humans didn't acknowledge them either. Once in a while, someone threw them a piece of bread, but mostly they went unnoticed. The pigeons to me were a sign from Mom, from Kenny, that we were on the right path.

I found the Police Department substation located on the north side of the train station. The counter had a window, and I had to talk through the metal plate in the middle. After explaining the situation, the officer checked his computer system for any dealings with Kenny.

"No contact with Mr. Smith. We are federal police. You need to ask local," he said. At the front counter, the man circled the street named Gutleutstraße, where the local police department was located. It was walking distance from the train station. The receptionist had me take a seat and wait. The officer walked in, looking a little disheveled, his uniform shirt untucked like he had had a busy morning. He first went to speak with the receptionist, who must have told him I was American.

"Yes, can I help you?" he asked in English.

"I would like to find out information about my American nephew, who went missing and has recently been sighted here in Frankfurt, near the train station."

"What is his name?"

"Kenneth Lee Smith. We call him Kenny."

"Okay, hold on," he said and went back into the reception area. A short time later, he came back.

"Do you mean Kenneth Smith Two?"

"Yes, Kenneth Smith, the second."

"Yes, I have had three different meetings with him, but nothing recent since June."

"Six months ago? Okay, can you circle the places on this map?"

The officer took the map and circled areas around the train station, the Hauptwache. Using the locations and my training, I drew a triangle grid search of those areas. I didn't have GPS since our phones didn't work in Germany. I don't know if it was my promise to Mom or pure arrogance in my investigation abilities in a country where I didn't speak the language, in a city of over 700,000 people, using a paper map with three six-month-old clues, but I was determined that Kenny was going to be found.

It was a cold, sunny day, and the Hauptwache was beautiful. One could easily get lost in the beauty of Frankfurt. St. Catherine's Church shadowed a large outdoor area filled with people as music played in the square. Though the train station was underground, I stayed above ground, surrounded by statues and tourists.

I looked for homeless people gathered and there were plenty. I taught myself enough German to ask if they spoke English and said that I was looking for my missing nephew. The first man we found was an older man sitting in a doorway with a sweet dog.

"Sprichst du Englisch?" I asked him.

"Nein," he said, shaking his head.

"Ich suche meinen vermissten amerikanischen Neffen," I said, showing him the picture of Kenny.

"Nein." He shook his head again.

We heard the same response one after another. None of the homeless for a two-mile stretch acknowledged knowing or seeing Kenny. The day slipped by, and it was time to go back to the hotel.

The next day, another train ride into the city and more places to look. Inside the triangle search grid, in the Sachsenhausen area, were three food kitchens where the homeless could get a free meal. No one had seen Kenny. Then to Schaumainkai, where Kenny was once spotted at the outdoor flea markets. No one had seen him recently. I walked further down the road to a medical facility on Schulstraße. We went inside and asked a nurse if she knew Kenny, who'd last been seen there six months earlier. She spoke a little English, but a medical delivery driver translated for me.

"She says she doesn't know your nephew. But he was here for a minor ailment six months ago."

"Can she tell the reason for his visit?" I asked.

"Something related to his feet," the driver said.

167

"This is my name, phone number, and email address. Can you tell her to email me because our phones don't work here, if he comes back in?" I asked. I handed the card to the driver. The driver advised her of my request, and the nurse nodded her head yes.

The delivery driver told of another hospital farther down the road called University Hospital Frankfurt. He offered to give me a ride. He took my business card and would email me if he saw Kenny. The University Hospital didn't have any information on Kenny either.

I tried to keep my emotions under control and remind myself that I was working the search like I would any other case and that I needed to be patient, but it's hard to separate your feelings when it's family, and you know in your bones that you're close to finding them. The nervous energy was exhausting me.

I returned to our hotel early because I needed to speak with the U.S. Consulate. From the first time I talked to Andrea Eggers, I liked her. She reminded me of the German version of myself—tough, no-nonsense, but fair. I made an appointment to meet in her office, located in downtown Frankfurt police headquarters. The clock continued to tick.

By our third day, the journey to the train station was routine. Every morning after an early breakfast at the hotel, we rode the shuttle to the airport, then I took the S Bahn train to Hauptbahnhof train station and walked. I walked so much my Fitbit nearly stopped working. A couple of streets from Hauptbahnhof station, there was a free kitchen where the homeless ate. The first kitchen had already closed, but we found an employee. She didn't speak English, but with my little bits of German, we were able to communicate. She hadn't seen Kenny.

I sat on the bench outside the kitchen and thought, if Kenny is not going to these kitchens and he's not in the hospital, where the hell is he? Maybe he's eating out of trash cans or found some friends, but that is probably a long stretch because Kenny's social skills would have been reduced down to nothing.

I went back to the bench outside the mission and sat in silence for a few minutes. Then I noticed that the pigeons aren't afraid of humans. The minutes turned to hours waiting for Kenny to appear at the homeless mission near Platform 1.

A plum, dark gray, and white pigeon walked over to me and looked up inquisitively as if it was trying to figure me out. I spoke to it, and it looked at me as if it was trying to understand. The German pigeon didn't look any different than the ones Mom raised in Missouri. She would throw seeds into the air, and the pigeons would flock to her. Some days Mom would prefer the company of the pigeons over us kids. She was like those pigeons. She roamed the land, free like them, kind of invisible without anyone to really acknowledge her existence.

I looked closer at the pigeon. It was missing two of its four talons. Remarkably, it was having no trouble walking across the dark tile train station floor. Even though the pigeon seemed helpless, he stood proudly. The pigeon was an amputee—like Kenny. The pigeon slid a little on the tile floor toward a piece of bread, and another pigeon came down and pushed the handicapped pigeon away. I wondered how Kenny protected himself on the streets in Frankfurt this long. I had seen too much from being a police officer and know what happens to homeless people; my stomach got sick when I thought of how people survived in the streets.

The kitchen opened for lunch, and after hours of waiting, Kenny was a no-show. The workers looked at the picture but didn't recognize him as a patron. They did provide some help and gave perfect directions to the last kitchen in the area. As I walked out of the kitchen toward the street, a pigeon flew beside us. I looked at the pigeon as another sign from Mom: maybe it was her guiding the investigation, assuring us to keep looking, or perhaps it was one of the pigeons flying to the afterlife to tell her I hadn't given up.

It was late in the afternoon when I reached the last kitchen. The building was filled with mostly older people who didn't speak English. I was directed to the manager, a middle-aged man, who could speak enough conversational English to translate. I showed him the picture of Kenny, and he passed it around to the 20 or so people in the building. He showed the picture to a table of older people eating lunch. One elderly woman, who spoke no English, became excited and told the interpreter something in German. He turned to us: "She says she sees him every morning in Hauptwache Station. She sees him every day. He is in a wheelchair..." the man said.

I learned Hauptwache in German refers to the central police station neighborhood. I hoped somewhere in Kenny's lost and damaged mind he was staying near the police because I would eventually show up. Police work was my life, my identity, and my inner sense of being.

I was excited for the 10 a.m. meeting with Ms. Eggers to share my results with her. I'd hoped the Consulate would now help me. I decided to splurge and spent 50 euros on a taxi to Kleyerstraße 86. The receptionist told me to have a seat, and Ms. Eggers would come and get me.

Ms. Eggers is a smaller, sturdy woman with glasses and strawberry blonde hair. Although she wasn't a police officer, she had my same sense of pride in her work. We sat down in her office, and she made me a lovely cup of tea. I showed her the pictures of Kenny and his tattoos. She said that they had contact with him on the street, but they hadn't seen him for six months. He wouldn't tell them why he was in Germany and often told lies or babbled in a language that didn't make any sense. She verified he was in a wheelchair with a thick beard and long hair. She confirmed that Kenny was usually in the Hauptwache station area—the same area we visited on our first day in Frankfurt.

About six months ago, her department had tried to put him on a plane to send him back to the United States, but he had body lice, and the pilot wouldn't allow him on the flight. I gave her copies of the pictures I had of him. Ms. Eggers advised me that the police could send officers to help in the search. She gave us her card with the two officers' cell phone numbers on the back. If Kenny was found, I was to contact the office or ask someone to call the police, and they would help get him to the airport. I left her office with a renewed sense of hope. I continued on to the train station beside her office and bought a ticket to Hauptwache station.

I had to ride the U train. I grabbed a map of the rail station lines and noticed something: all the stops around Hauptwache were handicapped-accessible. Kenny could get around easily. The trail was getting warmer.

Hauptwache's underground station was like many European train stations with a mix of restaurants, stores, and even a hair salon. An older gentleman was busking with a violin. This was a long way from rural southeast Missouri. I spotted a disheveled man with a scruffy beard and dirty clothes, carrying a backpack and a plain paper sack with a bottle shape inside. He reminded me of Kenny's absentee biological father.

"Heh, *Sprichst du Englisch?*" I asked, approaching him, smelling the aroma of alcohol.

"Yes, I speak a little English," he replied. I noticed his hands trembling. I had seen this before in dealing with people suffering from alcoholism.

"Have you seen this man?" I asked.

He studied the picture and said, "Rollstuhl. This is Rollstuhl. He is here and sleeps in front of the Bank of America at night. But stay here. He will be here soon."

"Where is the Bank?" I asked.

"The Bank of America is on Neue Mainzer Street," the man said. I took out the paper city map and had him circle the location. It was within a ten-minute walk.

"Who is Rawllstruit?" I asked.

"Rollstuhl, Rollstuhl." The man took his arms and put both of them in a motion as if he was pushing a wheelchair. Ah, *rollstuhl* was the German word for wheelchair. I gave him a couple of euros for his help.

"If you see him come find me. Here is the number for my hotel." I gave him one of the business cards for the hotel. I wrote my name on the back of the card.

"I will. I will. Rollstuhl is here. Stay here. He will be back."

The man took me to the middle of the station. More pigeons... As one flew to the right, I saw two things that made me know I was in the right place—an elevator and a Kentucky Fried Chicken restaurant.

171

I sat inside the KFC and watched out the window for Kenny. I was too worried to eat, but I found a table by the window. I kept a vigilant watch for Kenny. I soon started to feel frustrated. I just wanted a resolution. I stood up and said to myself, "I can't just sit here. I am going outside for some air."

I walked out into the hallway. I spotted a wheelchair coming fast toward me. As the wind moved the scruffy dangling beard of the driver, I saw the tattooed word "FIREWOOD." It was Kenny. He wheeled toward me. My heart raced and I grabbed the handles on the back of the wheelchair.

"Kenny, Kenny… it's Aunt Betty," I said as I held on tight to the wheelchair handles.

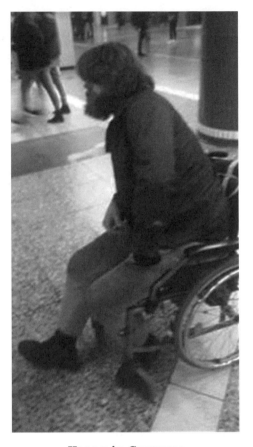

Kenny in Germany

Kenny looked strange, like he was searching the surrounding air for the answer to a question. I bent down and moved Kenny's beard to the side, checking for the neck tattoo.

"Kenny. It's me," I said as I bent over and looked him in his face.

Kenny just stared ahead. I pulled out the packet of pictures and showed them to him.

"Kenny, that is you with Jimmy and our son, Julian." Kenny stared at the photos and pointed to a picture of Julian. The first words he said:

"That is Julian. Aunt Betty, what are you doing here?"

"I've been looking for you."

Kenny's clothes were dirty. The tattoos he took so much pride in were now faded from being unprotected in the weather. His wheelchair was old and rusty. The shoes tied around his ankles had holes in the heels from his scooting his chair. His hair was longer than I have ever seen, and his face was covered by a long beard. The German police told me he had lice the last time they had contact with him. But his hair was clean and did not look like it had any lice nits in it. He wore smudged, dirty, dark black glasses, so dirty that I don't know how he saw out of them.

I asked the security guard to contact the officers who had been searching for Kenny. A couple of minutes later, two younger plainclothes police officers arrived. They looked like they should have been students in my Criminology 101 class. Dressed all in black clothes, with a jacket patch of a menacing bird with the feathers folding in the arms as if it was flexing its muscles.

"Are you Ms. Frizzell?" the dark-haired officer asked.

"Yes. That is me."

"Is this your nephew? Mr. Smith? How did you find Mr. Smith? We have been looking for him since the 22nd of June. You don't speak German, and Frankfurt is a big city."

With all my American pride and boisterousness, I replied, "This is how we do police work in the U.S."

The police instructed Kenny he needed to leave the country with me. Kenny got defiant. "I am not going back without a court order."

The officer explained to him, "This is not your country. You are here illegally. You will go to jail if you don't leave with your aunt."

"Take me to jail. I don't want to go back to the U.S."

I pleaded with Kenny.

"Kenny, come back with us. You don't have to go to Missouri. You can come to Seattle with us."

Kenny acted as if he was going in and out of consciousness. He would stop and start speaking in another unknown language unrecognizable to the German officers and me. Sometimes he put

173

his hand over his lips, turned to the left, and began a conversation with the air. The light-haired officer asked me what he was saying. I didn't know. It was some language beyond my high school sophomore French or my two years of middle school Spanish, or even the basic Spanish I managed to learn during my years with the police force.

"We can take you back to the hotel," the dark-haired officer said. The officers escorted Kenny on the elevator. We met them upstairs and on the street. A big van with *Polizei* on the side pulled into the alley. A large plainclothes officer closer to my age approached me.

"Ms. Frizzell, this is our chief."

A handsome, tall, muscular man extended his hand to me: "Ms. Frizzell, your investigation skills are quite impressive. Would you like to come work for us?" he asked, smiling.

"No, sorry, I already have a job. I just want my nephew home."

He smiled and nodded.

The younger officers helped Kenny get into the van. Kenny sat in back with the chief. Unlike U.S. police vans, there was no barred cage separating passengers from the German police van's driver. I sat with another younger officer in the front seat.

"You're an American police officer?" the officer asked.

"I was. Now I am an investigator for the state I live in."

"I can see you know how to conduct investigations."

I sighed, more from exhaustion than anything else, "Solving cases is my profession; I have many awards and certificates on my wall proving my skills but finding my nephew was a matter of life and death."

On the ride to the hotel, I tried to remind Kenny of happy times in his life, such as how much he loves my Denver omelet, or adventures he and Jimmy shared. Arriving at the hotel, the chief told me, "If you need anything, please call." He gave me his cell phone number.

I took Kenny to the hotel and used the elevator to our room. Once in our room, I gave him some of Jimmy's old clothes—a pair of pants and a T-shirt. While Kenny was taking his shower,

I threw his old rags for clothes in the trash. Then I called the Consulate, and they gave us the first appointment at 7 a.m. for an emergency passport. I bought Kenny a ticket on the same plane wc were booked on.

Kenny was noticeably quiet. He didn't ask about Vicky. I didn't ask him a lot of questions. He told me he lost his feet because he wore poisonous socks in Italy. He said he stayed with a German family who listened to music and drank hot tea.

After dinner, we went back to the room. I didn't sleep at all that night. I watched Kenny drink pot after pot full of tea. I knew that even if you love someone, they may not have control over impulses that make them do things they wouldn't want to, especially someone diagnosed with suicidal or homicidal ideation. For both of our safety, I stayed awake. Half the night, he just watched TV, or he would talk to a nonexistent person to his left. Occasionally, he would take out a notebook and pen to write things in it. At one point around 3 a.m., Kenny and his unseen companion got into a heated discussion. I showed him a picture of Mom, and he stared at it for a while, and that managed to stop him from talking.

The little boy from the front yard doing bird calls with his hands was now a profoundly disabled adult man stuck in a destructive narrative created by his mind. I studied him for hours as he sat in the chair; he slipped in and out of reality with each passing minutc. Finally, breakfast came at 5 a.m. and then the train ride to the Consulate. I made sure we did not ride through Hauptwache if he or his impalpable friend thought of disappearing back to the streets.

We arrived at the Consulate and waited in a long line to be checked. They searched us and put our cell phones and personal property in a locked bin. We took an elevator to the second floor and waited for them to call our name. Once we were called, I paid the money for Kenny's passport. They told us to remain in the lobby. The hours ticked away, and the time got closer to our plane taking off.

Finally, the lady called only me back to the room. Kenny was asleep in his chair.

"Ms. Frizzell, we can't issue Mr. Smith a passport. He has an arrest warrant from Stoddard County, Missouri," she said in a sympathetic tone.

"That is impossible. The prosecutor told everyone, including Kenny's attorney, that charge went away when he testified."

She showed me the warrant. The warrant wasn't for theft; it was for forgery. I asked her to go to the State of Missouri circuit court online system to get more details. The theft charge had been closed and removed but now Stoddard County charged Kenny with forgery, an entirely new case. The warrant was issued while Kenny was lost in Germany. The Consulate tried to get special permission to waive the rules and issue the passport, but we were out of time. I had to leave, or we would miss our flight.

Now, after all this work, Kenny was left helpless and homeless in the street. A pigeon wandering aimlessly on the tile of the train station. Nobody sees him, nobody cares.

I walked back to the area as Kenny sat in his chair, sleeping.

"You can't go home with us. You have a warrant out of Stoddard County." The words fell from my mouth.

Kenny awoke from a nap. Twisting in his wheelchair turning to me, he said, "Warrants can be taken care of. You can take care of it."

"No, no. I can't," I screamed in my head. For the first time in his 34 years of life, I could not help him. Stoddard County, Missouri, saw me as a loudmouth, white trash sister of a murderer, not as an expert and experienced former Chief of Police turned social justice advocate. Hadn't Stoddard County done enough to the people I love? Vicky sat over five thousand miles away in a Missouri prison, doing life plus 25 years for murder. My name was vilified by the media-seeking prosecutor who went to the local news telling lies out of spite. Why? Because I didn't have the "right" name? Because I am a woman and I don't have a voice in that part of Missouri? Or because the corrupted system of justice had become hardened and callous, and removed any notion of human decency from their proceedings. The quality of mercy wasn't strained; it didn't exist.

176

"No. I am going to have to fly back without you. The plane leaves in an hour." My voice was struggling to get out over the throb of my heartbeat in my throat. I dug out all the euros from my pocket and purse and threw them on Kenny's lap. He took the money and put it in his bag.

"You have my number?" I said, breathing heavily and holding back tears.

"Yes," he replied, trying to wake up more.

"The consulate worker will be out here in a minute. We will be fuckin' back for you."

I walked quickly to the elevator. Not looking back. I couldn't. If I saw him in his rusty used wheelchair, unkempt hair and beard, wearing Jimmy's old clothes, I'd collapse there. I rationalized the only chance he had was for me to get back to the States and fight for the miserable warrant to be dismissed. As soon as the black elevator doors opened, the world went wet and white. I fell crying on the sterile floor. I don't cry. Crying is a sign of weakness. Crying makes me angry. I want to hit something or someone. I needed to be out of the security-heavy consulate now.

Exiting the consulate, I didn't care about the security. They asked me if I was all right.

"Hell no, I am not all right. I haven't been all right since 2013."

The older security guard handed me my phone and ID. Usually, I would have talked to him, but now I just wanted out of there before I lost myself altogether and did something violent fueled by the rage and anger rising up in my blood, rising up in my mother's blood.

Women in my family equate pain with anger. The urge to punch something overcame me. Anger turned to despondency. Kenny can't come home. I couldn't stop crying. The ride to the airport was too long. My cries broke the silence of the ride. Leaving Kenny was causing Jimmy pain too. Occasionally, I wiped my eyes and looked at Jimmy also quietly crying, respectfully clearing his eyes.

I was defeated. The taxi driver who spoke little English was probably glad to get rid of us two crying American fools. I was numb. I don't remember going through security or even boarding the plane.

During the plane ride home, I felt I couldn't do anything but cry. We had a layover in Iceland. The bitter cold air felt good to my tear-stung cheeks. I hadn't eaten since breakfast, and my diabetes told me I *had* to eat. As I began chewing, the calmer and clearer my thinking became. Kenny was going to get home, maybe not by Thanksgiving in two weeks, but at least by Christmas. A terrible windstorm approached as we boarded our plane. We sat on the plane waiting to take off, and the Icelandic wind spoke to me in Mom's voice, telling me, "You don't give up."

There was so much to be done, and I couldn't do it alone. I made a list of the hundreds of minor things and the dozens of major items that needed to be resolved. I was grateful to live in Washington state, where my Senator Maria Cantwell's office was supportive and helpful in helping me cut through the bureaucratic red tape. Still, I needed to deal with Stoddard County, Missouri myself.

I spoke to Kenny's public defender supervisor, Chris Davis, who said the attorney who had the case no longer worked for the office. Mr. Davis was familiar with Kenny's case and was surprised to hear about a new charge; he was under the same impression as Kenny and the bondsman—that all charges against him were dismissed when he gave his deposition against Vicky. He said he would look into Kenny's case to see if there was anything they needed from Vicky.

Vicky phoned for her usual weekend call. She was anxious to hear about the trip to Germany and whether I found Kenny. After telling her the sad tale, she was depressed.

"Why don't they just come after me? Leave Kenny alone," she said.

"I don't know, sis. Probably because Chris' family is pushing it. Has anyone from the public defender's office taken a statement from you?"

"No. No one has talked to me."

It was a mystery to everyone except the Stoddard County Sheriff's office why they were pursuing forgery charges against a mentally ill homeless man.

I called the Consulate nightly. The Frankfurt police were keeping tabs on Kenny to ensure he didn't disappear again. On the day before Thanksgiving, the Consulate informed me that a limited travel passport was approved for Kenny to travel to Seattle. The passport was valid for three days of travel back to the United States. It was the only lifeline we had, and we took it. I had used all my vacation days on the last trip to Germany, so the plan was that Jimmy would go alone to Frankfurt on December 6th and return on December 8th—with Kenny.

The days waiting felt like weeks. On November 28th, I spoke at the Rural Criminal Justice summit held at Deason Law School in Dallas, Texas. I presented about mental health and the rural police departments. I talked about my professional experiences, and I also shared my personal experiences with Vicky's and Kenny's cases. I learned more about the terrible prospects for the poor who turned to crime in Missouri. A representative from the Vera Institute of Justice (a nationwide group working to reform bail practices that criminalize poverty) shared statistics that the highest number of new Missouri inmates were from the rural areas, not, as most people assume, from the urban areas of St. Louis and Kansas City. Another expert cited that the number of women inmates had tripled in the last decade and that Missouri was one of the states with the highest growth rates in female incarceration. My family was living proof of their statistics.

On December 4, 2018, Jimmy went back to Germany to get Kenny. We treated the trip as if it were a spy mission. I wrote step-by-step instructions with photographs of the area, and programmed numbers into his Skype account on his phone. The Consulate made the arrangements to drop Kenny's emergency passport off at the hotel. Ms. Eggers coordinated with the Frankfurt police to take Kenny to the airport and ensure he got through customs and on the plane. I packed new clothes and shoes in his bag for Kenny. Jimmy would use Skype to communicate with me, the Consulate, and the German authorities.

The hours ticked by, but finally, two hours after Jimmy's plane landed, I received a Skype message, "I have Kenny." Jimmy told me that the German police had been in constant contact with Kenny since I found him and let him know that we were coming to get him. According to Jimmy, Kenny was happy to see him.

The Consulate spoke to Kenny to get his verbal assurance, as much as he could, that he wanted to go back to the United States with Jimmy. They knew the legal guardianship paperwork was in process, but this was such an unusual case that the protocol for handling this type of deportation was unprecedented. Kenny told them he was ready to come home. For the next day, Kenny slept, only getting up to eat and use the restroom. Jimmy called to video chat. I could see Kenny sitting in his chair in the background writing in a book.

"What has he been doing?"

"Just writing in his book and drinking tea."

From our video chat, I could see Kenny look up and acknowledge me for a minute, then go back to writing in the book.

"The U.S. Consulate will be here the morning we leave with the emergency passport. The Frankfurt police set up a time to drive us to the airport."

The evening before their plane was to leave, Jimmy called me while Kenny was in the shower.

"Kenny said something to me and I really don't know how to react."

"Jimmy, you know he is off his meds. But what did he say?"

"First, he told me he was sexually and physically assaulted in the Stoddard County Jail. He wanted to claim sanctuary in Germany because he was in fear of retaliation from Stoddard County. Then out of nowhere, he said, 'Firewood is dead. I am August McDougal.' I just let him talk and didn't ask questions. I just agreed with him. Also, when he registered in the hotel, he put his nationality as Italian."

"Well, he needs his medicine," I said.

"That is not the only medicine he needs. He has body lice on his clothes. I took them and threw them in the garbage outside, and he has worm-like things coming out of the wounds on his back."

"Oh, no. We *have* to make sure he is on that plane. We'll take him to the emergency room as soon as you all land."

"Okay. We will be on the plane in a couple hours."

"Okay. I am going to sleep. Text me from the airport."

My heart sank thinking of Kenny having a million different diseases. I was already thinking about filing a lawsuit on the alleged abuse in Stoddard County. Only a few months ago, the misogynistic Stoddard County Jail administrator, whom I had spoken to early in Vicky's case, was arrested for rape.[1]

I awoke a short time later to my phone ringing.

"Hello."

"Kenny is not on the plane with me... He disappeared..."

"What? What happened?" I was trying to wake up.

"Two hours before the plane was to take off, he told me he was going downstairs to check the internet and go to the restroom. I went down a few minutes later, I went down there, and he was gone. The lobby clerk said he was on the computer. I checked the history, and he looked up the status of his Stoddard County case and how to file sanctuary status. The Frankfurt police looked for him. But couldn't find him. I am sorry."

"Just come home," I said. I felt numb. I didn't have any more heart to break.

Vicky called the next day, hoping to speak with Kenny. I sensed her disappointment when she learned he ran off again.

"He'll come home when he wants to. I will just pray on it," she

---

1 He was convicted. https://www.wpsdlocal6.com/archive/stoddard-county-jail-administra-tor-charged-with-rape/article_e79f8bdb-ac4c-5f68-b8b8-d34d89da7ac0.html

said. She didn't understand that he was never coming home. I didn't tell her about the abuse Kenny suffered in jail. It would have been too much for one day.

"That is all we can do," I told her.

I wrapped myself in the silence and darkness, thinking of the promise to Mom. "I tried, Mom... I tried," I said, shaking my head.

Legally, my hands are tied. I couldn't force Kenny back to the United States because I didn't have custody of him. I didn't have custody of him because he has to be present in court, but he couldn't be in court because he was in Germany. No one was willing to reopen the murder case. Vicky, with her misplaced guilt, refused to change her story. Any of the physical evidence of the case, like Kenny's clothing, was long gone. The gun was never tested for his fingerprints or DNA.

It was sad to think that he was safer living homeless on the streets of a foreign country than in the Missouri county he lived most of his life. Yet, his deteriorating physical condition would determine how long and how well he could survive on the Frankfurt streets. The German government still wanted to deport him back to the United States, but they're not actively trying to force a mentally ill and disabled man onto a plane. In any other jail but Stoddard County, Kenny might have the chance at getting the medical attention he desperately needs for both his physical and mental ailments.

I promised Mom nearly 20 years ago to take care of Vicky and Kenny, but no one ever promised to take care of me. There comes a time one has to stop chasing the ghosts of the past and start living life in the present. For the first time ever, I was going to take care of myself. I took advice from Vicky and put my faith in God to resolve the Kenny situation. If I wasn't healthy, I couldn't help those who needed me the most—my son and me.

I would continue to fight for Vicky and Kenny, but I needed to fight for myself too. I know Mom would be proud of my efforts. I could hear her say, "If anyone can get things done, it is you, Betty Jane."

I tried and will keep trying.

CHAPTER TWELVE

There used to be a drive-in movie theater located outside of Poplar Bluff. A blue and white neon sign blinked off and on the marquee of the movie titles. Mom would have the younger kids hide under a blanket in the backseat of the car, so she didn't have to pay admission. We never had the money for popcorn, but Mom would bring snacks from home for us. The hot, humid Missouri nights dusted in mosquitoes made watching an outdoor movie oftentimes unbearable, but being around people was always a treat.

Next to the drive-in was the Westwood country club; it was the fancy golf course and country club in Poplar Bluff. A place no one in my family would ever have a chance to walk into. From the drive-in, you could scc into the building where the members dined and had drinks. Each table was set with a beautiful tablecloth. Families, the ones I consider real families, with a father, mother, and children, ate off clean, shiny, matching plates, and there was lots of food. No one was fighting for the last piece of chicken.

I was more interested in what was going on at the country club than the boring rerun of an old *Planet of the Apes* movie. I wondered why I didn't have a life like that. Why didn't I have a father? Why didn't I live in a house? Why didn't Mom smile like that mother sitting at the fancy table? That day, I promised myself I would have a family and life just like the families at the country club.

I realized my dream of the clean, happy family life I had when I was young wasn't the dream I had as an adult. Therapy taught me how to handle the changes that life brought, and accept both the sadness and the happiness that comes from growth. My son, Julian, put it into perspective by saying, "You can't expect the same people who stayed with you when you were sick to stay with you when you are well."

Therapy also helped me to find a way to come to terms with Vicky's prison sentence. Her entire life lived in a rural county, with the lack of schooling and health resources, contributed mightily to

Vicky and Me, Chillicothe Correctional Center, 2019

her tragedy. If she had been closer to one of the limited Missouri mental health courts, perhaps she would be getting rehabilitation instead of years in a prison cell. However, she was now safe from the abuses she suffered in the outside world. No good will come from putting a severely abused woman with diminished intelligence in a prison when her life outside was worse than any penitentiary.

I will always feel the wrong person is in jail for this crime. That is not the justice I served when I wore a uniform for so many years. I wasn't out on patrol, missing Christmases and birthdays with my family, to see the criminal justice system bastardized in this way. I'm still angry at how my family and the thousands of families like mine have been treated by rural law enforcement and legal systems.

Kenny is still in Frankfurt, Germany. He continues to suffer from schizophrenia. The Frankfurt police send me regular updates and the Consulate would like to send him back to the United States, but to whom and to what end? Kenny is imprisoned by his mental illness and the abuse at the hands of a vindictive Sheriff's Department. The Bible may say "An eye for an eye," but if that is our only response to crime, then we are at risk of the entire world becoming blinded to thousands of terrible things that lead a person to commit an act of theft, fraud, violence.

Four years after Vicky was sentenced to life in prison, we both have found one thing that had eluded us our entire life—happiness. How miserable was Vicky's life to find joy in living in prison? Like in one of our childhood Bible stories, Vicky may feel she is finally a good mother by paying penance for a crime she didn't commit. Vicky teaches Bible study to younger inmates and is working toward an associate degree in theology. Every time she calls, she has a new story or adventure to share, because she is living. It took losing her physical freedom to find true freedom.

Jimmy too found his happiness. He moved back to Missouri. I set him up with an acquaintance of mine from high school and they found love.

Therapy helped me learn to love myself and ultimately learn to love someone else. One night, after my marriage ended, I took

Julian to see a friend's band in Seattle. Then I saw him—Mom would have called him a "tall, cool drink of water." I told Julian, "I think that drummer is cute." Julian told me to go talk to him. "No way, I don't chase men," I said. Even though I was in the Pacific Northwest, I still held on to my Southern girl ways. But we did start talking. He's a bit older but we had a lot in common—both were coming out of lengthy marriages, have sons, and love music. Mom used to say, "I would rather be an older man's sweetheart than a young man's fool."

Looking back at everything, I am reminded of Mom and one of her stories. Mom was about seven years old, living deep in the thick woods bordering the Mark Twain National Forest. Grandma Roxie sent Mom outside to the coop to feed the chickens and gather eggs. The wind picked up, and the sky turned black. Mom heard a loud rumble followed by wind and dust. A Missouri tornado came directly at Mom. She dropped the eggs and started running toward the house. As she opened the screen door, the wind tore it from its hinges. Mom grabbed the door. She held on tight as the wind carried both her and the door away down deep into the woods, where she landed far from the sight of her house. Scratched and bruised but alive, she got up and praised God. She was alive.

I realized my life had been in a storm since 2013. We were all caught up in the wind and dust of the cyclone of poverty and mental illness. They uprooted my life and twisted everything about. With them came the debris of the murder case and mental health breakdowns that consumed and nearly suffocated me. The rural county criminal justice system was like the meanest tornado of all, twisting and turning my days until I didn't know where I would end up. My family is my screen door, my strength and stability. I made it. I am still here, breathing, loving, and living— hurt and a little bruised, but here to love and fight another day.

>≈<

Thank You

I would like to acknowledge the eastside of Poplar Bluff and the alums of J. Minnie Smith School for making me the person I am today. *Eastside for life.*

I would like to thank Dawn Dupler for her expertise and guidance. Ashley Victoria Taylor for the photos. Dolores Shearon, we came close to being an actual family but we will always be eastside family. Betty Absheer for being a role model. I strive to be half the influence you were on my life. Jolene Kingery for being that teacher everyone wants in their classroom. Pamela Des Barres for her workshops and encouragement to finally "finish" my story. Susan Kolliopoulos and Nicole Cormaci for their willingness to read and advice. FBI Special Agent Michael Johnson for showing me integrity in law enforcement.